God's Pitcher

And Other Spiritual Thoughts

God's Pitcher

And Other Spiritual Thoughts

Volume One
Wisdom for Life Series
Devotional Books for Women

Gloria Baird

DPI
DISCIPLESHIP
PUBLICATIONS
INTERNATIONAL

www.dpibooks.org

God's Pitcher and Other Spiritual Thoughts
© 2008 by Discipleship Publications International
5016 Spedale Court #331
Spring Hill, TN 37174

All Scripture quotations, unless indicated, are taken fromthe NEW
INTERNATIONAL VERSION. Copyright ©1973, 1978, 1984 by the
International Bible Society. Used by permission of Zondervan
Publishing House. All rights reserved.

The "NIV" and "New International Version" trademarks are regis-
tered in the United States Patent Trademark Office by the
International Bible Society. Use of either trademark requires the permission of the International Bible Society.

Printed in the United States of America

ISBN: 978-1-57782-230-1

Cover Design: Brian Branch
Interior Design: Thais Gloor
Front cover photo: ©iStockphotos/AndrewGentry

To my children and grandchildren

You were the inspiration for me to share my walk.
"I have no greater joy than to hear that my
children are walking in the truth."
3 John 4

Contents

Other Writings

❀

Foreword

❀

Dear Reader,

As I write this, you may imagine me, breathing a long sigh of relief.

Battle won.

Your holding this book demonstrates that the "important" has vanquished the "urgent," and with it, all other worthy and unworthy distractions that might well have kept Gloria Baird from writing this book, and you from reading it.

I think it was about eight years ago, the first time I heard the germ of the idea for this book. It came from a group of Christian women who worked together in an office, and who had enjoyed the blessing of being in a discipleship group with Gloria every Thursday morning at 8:00 AM before their workday began. It rather amazed me how much they all got out of the group. It was not an ideal set-up. After fighting the morning rush hour, twenty to thirty women would gather in a conference room, all wanting to tell good news or share struggles of the week, or ask for input about marriage or children or singlehood or offer a prayer request.

With only forty-five minutes together—maximum— how much effective personal attention would you really expect to get out of a group like that? It was Gloria's "pitcher analogy" in action. She allowed her unique self to be filled up on a regular basis, through her daily study of God's word, prayer and God's faithful discipling of her through relationships and all life's circumstances; and then she faithfully poured out what she was learning, understanding and experiencing each week with those women. She managed it in such a relatable way, they all testified that in those few short minutes they spent together each week, they had been changed—for good.

If you've picked up this book, you probably already trust that the message of God's wisdom is unspeakably powerful. And yet, not every messenger is able to deliver it in such a way that it sinks into your heart. *God's Pitcher and Other Spiritual Thoughts* is, without a doubt, all about the message. I would, however, wish for you to know that Gloria Baird is a remarkable and trustworthy messenger. She's a bona fide, spiritual maven. ("Maven" is Yiddish for "one who accumulates knowledge.") In his bestseller entitled *The Tipping Point*, Malcolm Gladwell describes the role of a maven in this way:

> When people are overwhelmed with information and develop immunity to traditional forms of communication, they turn instead for advice and information to the people in their lives whom they respect, admire, and trust.[1]

In other words, a maven doesn't just latch onto a great message; she lives out the message in such a compelling way that it becomes contagious, and, like a happy epidemic, spreads good change. Then the good changes stick from person to person, producing the kind of lasting and meaningful impact that I believe we all would love to leave as a legacy.

Gloria is a maven of matrimony: her forty-seven-year marriage to Al Baird is consistently and intimately romantic, dynamic, fresh, outwardly focused and inspiring. All of us who have heard and followed her marriage advice from the Bible know our marriages are unquestionably better for it.

She is a maven of motherhood: her three daughters are faithful, committed disciples of Jesus Christ, married to faithful, committed disciples, and at this writing, her first granddaughter has just been baptized into Christ.

1. Malcolm Gladwell, *The Tipping Point* (New York: Little, Brown and Company, 2000), 275.

She's a maven of the marvelous message of God's wisdom for this hurting world in which we live: no stranger to tragedy or hard times (as a young woman, burying three of her children; as a women's ministry leader and elder's wife, serving in a fast-growing international fellowship of churches and often being brought in to help with all the ugliest, the worst, the most depressing and disheartening counseling situations), she remains one of the most sincerely and consistently happy, gracious, contented, relatable women I have ever known.

Gloria would probably tell you that the main reason she felt compelled to write this book was to make sure she passed on these valuable personal spiritual insights to her children and grandchildren. A noble ambition, and certainly more than a good enough reason to put pen to paper.

Let's make sure we take the wisdom still further. Whatever resonates with us from these pages, or whatever the Holy Spirit may teach us personally, may we pour it out generously to others.

> She speaks with wisdom,
>   and faithful instruction is on her tongue.
>   Proverbs 31:26

Tammy Fleming
Birmingham, England
July 2008

1

God's Pitcher

> May the God of hope fill you with all joy and peace as you trust in him, so that you may overflow with hope by the power of the Holy Spirit.
>
> Romans 15:13

God, the potter, shapes us as clay into various vessels for his use. If God were to allow me to choose what vessel I would like to be, I would choose to be a pitcher. A pitcher, like a vase or a glass, is designed to be filled. However, a pitcher has a spout so that whatever is in it can be poured out.

What fills the pitcher is of prime concern; no one would be attracted to a pitcher filled with poison or some foul-smelling liquid. The purpose of the pitcher is to be emptied. It has a handle on it because it needs someone to do the pouring. It is important for the pitcher to be clean on the inside before it is filled. If the pitcher is dirty, its contents are tainted and undesirable.

One of my favorite gifts to give as a wedding present is a crystal pitcher. A crystal pitcher is especially useful because it is clear, transparent—you can see what is on the inside.

As I think of being a "pitcher" to be used by God, I see the necessity of being cleansed through the blood of Christ, and being continually washed, ready for use. Then I need to be still to allow God to fill me with his word and his Spirit, so that there is good that will overflow when God is ready to do the pouring.

God frequently uses the people around us to "grab the handle" and help the pouring process. This analogy comes to life for me as I begin writing this book. I know that God has taught me many things that have helped me through the years, but I also know that he wants me to share these lessons with others. It has been an easy overflow for me to talk about these as I teach and counsel others, but it has taken the urging of several people around me to do the extra pouring out in writing.

The clear, transparent quality of the crystal pitcher is a necessary ingredient for being used as God's pitcher.

Without being open about my insecurities and hesitancies, others would not know how to help and encourage me. In essence, I could allow my pitcher to be partially filled with those insecurities, and that would prevent God from totally filling it with whatever he desires.

Satan is eager to add to or take over the filling process with his lies. It is my choice to determine who will fill my pitcher. I must be willing to be emptied of myself to be filled by God.

What a challenge, but what a privilege to be God's pitcher!

2

The Turtle Syndrome

> You are my hiding place;
>> you will protect me from trouble
>> and surround me with songs of deliverance.
>>> Psalm 32:7

As we flew from Boston to Texas to spend Christmas with our family, I was preoccupied with anxious thoughts about my mother's health. She had recently had a bone marrow test but had not gotten the results. We were hoping and praying for a good report, but we also knew that the news is not always what you want to hear.

As I reflect on this time, I think it was one of the first times I seriously considered that I could lose my mother. With the depth of those feelings welling up in me, I began to prepare for the worst. I remember thinking that I needed to be strong and ready to handle whatever report we would face.

Thankfully, when we arrived, we got the news that her test results were good. I soon forgot about the tests and all my concerns and went on to enjoy the Christmas holidays.

However, on the trip back home I remember telling Al that I didn't seem to feel the same excitement and warmth that I usually felt in our times with the family. As I was trying to think through this experience, I remembered hearing someone say that we cannot just shut off our painful feelings without shutting off the good feelings as well. Then I realized that was what I had done. I had tried to "steel" myself so I wouldn't fall apart if there was bad news, but I had also "steeled" myself so I didn't feel the good things either. I had basically put myself in neutral.

That experience was the birth of my "turtle syndrome" analogy. I began to think about the way God gives the turtle a shell for its protection. But the turtle cannot eat or move unless its head and legs come out of the shell. The shell does keep out the bad, but it could also keep out the good. The turtle must be vulnerable in order to live.

Obviously, we are not turtles, and God did not give us shells for protection, yet we often try to protect ourselves.

We want to be in control especially in the area of our emotions. When feeling sad, we may try not to cry; when feeling weak, we may try to seem strong; when feeling lonely, we may try not to need anyone; when feeling tempted, we may try to hide it. Too often our deepest emotions are the ones we bury or mask under our "shell."

In a similar way that the turtle has to be vulnerable to live, we also have to be vulnerable to experience real life. God makes it possible for us to be vulnerable because he is our protector. In reading through the Psalms, I was amazed when I realized how many descriptions of God relate to protection: shield, refuge, stronghold, rock, fortress, deliverer, support, Savior, Redeemer, ever-present help, hiding place.

As I have come to be more aware of the protection God has promised for my life, I have been convicted that my self-protectiveness is sin. When I try to protect myself (not meaning being wise in locking my doors or not walking alone in dark alleys), I am trying to take over God's role. My lack of faith that God will really do what he promised moves me to try to take control.

I have to decide to trust God and be totally vulnerable with him. To me that means expressing my feelings and completely surrendering to him. When I can trust God to be my protector, it is much easier to be vulnerable with the people around me.

Vulnerability breeds vulnerability, helping me to see that others have similar struggles. Out of my shell, I can actually feel safer and more bonded with others than ever!

3

But God

"You intended to harm me, *but* God intended it to to accomplish what is now being done, the saving of many lives."

Genesis 50:20 (emphasis added)

"I would like to accept your invitation, but…"
"That is a good idea, but…"
"I want to do the right thing, but…"

Frequently in our conversations we hear this word, and we may cringe, waiting for what comes next. The conjunction "but" usually introduces a differing view, an opposite direction or contrasting thought. Some of these "buts" may be insignificant, while others have life-changing consequences.

Too often the "but" is followed with excuses such as, "I would like to be a different person, but because of my difficult past, I cannot change." Our past experiences, mistakes or failures sometimes grab on to us, and we have a difficult time being freed of them. I have heard that most of us fall into one of two categories—we are either accused or deceived. I can identify with the accused personality, easily feeling guilty for something I should have done and did not do, or for doing or saying something that I should not have done or said.

As I write this, I can almost feel that sinking feeling that comes over me at those times. While it is vital to take responsibility for our actions, it is destructive to let the past dictate who we are. We can "beat ourselves up" for mistakes we have made, essentially chaining ourselves to our past.

Recently as I reread the account of Joseph and his brothers in Genesis 37–50, I was stopped by a verse I had quickly read over. In Genesis 45 Joseph identified himself to his brothers as their brother whom they had sold into slavery, then lied to their father, telling him that Joseph had been killed by a wild animal. Imagine their shock. They were terrified at his presence!

Joseph's response to their fear in Genesis 45:5 caught my attention in a deeper way than ever before:

"And now, do not be distressed and do not be angry with yourselves for selling me here, because it was to save lives that God sent me ahead of you."

His brothers definitely had a past, and it had caught up with them. At that moment their jealous actions of the past weighed heavily on them. Probably they were in the process of "beating themselves up." Joseph recognized their pain and told them not to be angry with themselves for what they had done. That was certainly an unexpected, yet welcomed response. After all the damage Joseph's brothers had done to him, how could he not be bitter toward them?

There was more to the story than Joseph's being sold into slavery. Joseph had seen God's hand move through his life in many powerful ways bringing good out of hard situations. He trusted God's big picture of his life. One of Joseph's strongest statements of faith was in these words to his brothers:

"You intended to harm me, *but* God intended it for good to accomplish what is now being done, the saving of many lives." (Genesis 50:20, emphasis added)

When you are tempted to hold yourself a prisoner to your past, remember the life-changing words—"*but God*...." There is so much more to your life than is evidenced by the isolated occurrences you experience. God is weaving the tapestry of your life; you may see only the knots and loose ends on the back of the canvas, *but God* sees his cohesive masterpiece.

4

❦

The Whirlpool Syndrome

❧

And whatever you do, whether in word or
deed, do it all in the name of the Lord Jesus,
giving thanks to God the Father through him.
Colossians 3:17

Have you ever noticed that one negative thought
seems to feed another negative thought? I have a vivid
picture in my mind of a time when this happened to me.
I must have taken great pride in being sure my family had
clean clothes in their drawers because I was appalled
when my husband, Al, let me know he was out of clean
socks!

At that moment I felt like a derelict wife—and, of
course, the fact that his drawer was empty of clean socks

proved that my thinking was right on target!

It wasn't long till something happened with one of our girls (I can't even remember what it was), and I immediately started thinking that I was a terrible mother.

Then I thought of something I had failed to do for one of my friends, which proved that I wasn't a good friend either. The next thought that followed was "I'm not much of a Christian, and I'm not so sure how God feels about me right now."

Talk about negative thinking! In a few minutes I was in the pits. My thinking had spiraled downward out of control—all because of a pair of socks, or lack thereof!

I wish I could say that was the only time I experienced such destructive thinking, but it was not an isolated happening. In fact, the pattern occurred often enough that I finally recognized and labeled it my "whirlpool syndrome." Being pulled down by the whirlpool left me feeling defeated, depressed and devoid of any energy.

The trigger for my negative thinking might vary, but the root cause usually was tied to something I didn't do well or something I had failed to do. In time I began to see that Satan is a master at being sure that something happens to prove that my negative thought is true, making my whirlpool seem inevitable.

The recognition that Satan was involved in my thinking

actually helped me to begin to change my whirlpool syndrome. Part of Jesus' description of the devil in John 8:44 clarifies the picture:

> "He was a murderer from the beginning, not holding to the truth, for there is no truth in him. When he lies, he speaks his native language, for he is a liar and the father of lies."

As soon as I can identify that Satan is working, I can label that thought a lie. The quick downward spiral of my thinking became a clue for me that Satan was active and that I needed to be alert and ready to fight back.

It has also helped me to ask myself the question, "Who would want me to think this way—God or Satan?" Usually the answer is obvious. I certainly do not want to believe a lie, so it makes me more determined to hold on to God's truth.

The quickest and most powerful weapon that I have found to use against Satan's negative pulls is thanksgiving. First of all, it is always right to be thankful. In addition, thanksgiving is a powerful antidote for sin, as seen in Ephesians 5:3–4:

> But among you there must not be even a hint of sexual immorality, or of any kind of impurity, or of greed, because these are improper for

God's holy people. Nor should there be obscenity, foolish talk or coarse joking, which are out of place, but rather *thanksgiving*. (emphasis mine)

At times when I have felt the whirlpool starting, I have flooded my mind with thankful thoughts, sometimes saying aloud all the things for which I am thankful. Thanksgiving immediately focuses on God and crowds out the devil and his negative lies.

Instead of the downward spiral of the whirlpool, thanksgiving reverses the whirlpool pulling upward toward God. The more quickly and frequently I can be thankful, the more victories I have experienced over my negative whirlpool syndrome.

5

Open Hands Prayer

I call to you, O LORD, every day;
   I spread out my hands to you.

Psalms 88:9

As I was driving in stop-and-go traffic, I felt myself tensing up and getting more and more anxious. I was running late for an appointment, and there was nothing I could do to move any faster. The longer I sat there, the tighter my hands gripped the steering wheel—I was really up-tight!

Finally, I started praying, "Lord, you know where I need to be—help me to trust you to get me there." I took a deep breath, relaxed my tense shoulders and loosened my hands from the steering wheel.

My open hands had my fingernail marks on them from my tight grip. It suddenly hit me that my being tense had accomplished nothing, but that praying and opening my hands had given me an instant peaceful feeling even in the midst of traffic.

That experience was the birth of my open-hands prayer.

Praying with open hands has become my expression in a physical way of trusting God and surrendering my will to his. This has become a common practice for me personally, but there are times when it is a real struggle for me to keep my hands open.

I remember a walk on the beach when I was agonizing over a situation (interestingly, I can't remember the specific situation, but I do remember the battle I was feeling within).

I was crying, praying and alternately opening my hands, then clenching my fists. I was fighting for control! Peace only comes when I open my hands and keep them open.

I often picture this struggle as similar to a toddler clenching a piece of candy in his hands while his mother is telling him to give the candy to her. It is only a losing battle for the toddler. He can hold on to the candy until he ruins it by melting it in his hands. Then he also has to deal with having to have his hands washed. No matter how hard he tries, his mother is stronger, and she can pry his little fingers away from the candy if she chooses.

He may be missing an even better treat; his mom may have planned to give him his favorite dessert after his dinner! How much better it would be for him if he opened up his hand, obeyed his mother and trusted her to give him what is best for him when it is best.

How are you with your "candy"—that husband you want, or that baby, or new home, or job…? By opening up our hands before God and putting that desire, concern or whatever in our hands without closing them, God then can leave it there, take it away, replace it with something better, or give it back at the best time. It is in his hands and under his control. I have found my greatest peace when my hands are open!

6

⚜

Action and Reaction

⚜

"...I have set before you life and death, blessings and curses. Now choose life."

Deuteronomy 30:19

When I was a young bride in Austin, Texas, I became aware of my need to have input from some older women. Fortunately, I had a strong relationship with my mother and was thankful for the advice and counsel I was able to get from her.

However, I also needed other women who could share lessons from their own lives. I remember asking the elders' wives if they could teach a class for some of the younger women. They quickly dismissed the idea since they didn't feel qualified to teach.

Some time after that a retired couple came to hold a workshop at the church we attended. The husband taught classes for the men, while his wife taught the women. The time she spent with the women has had an indelible impact on my life. She was an example of what I prayed that I could become—an older woman teaching and influencing younger women. Looking back, I can see that God used her to influence my role with younger women, and he used this couple as one of the first models to later shape the way Al and I would work together.

In addition to the example this older woman set, she taught a life lesson that I will never forget. She said, "It is not important what happens to you, but it is how you act and react to situations and persons and things that makes all the difference."

I heard that statement forty years ago, and yet it continues to ring in my ears, impacting me to this very day. Not only does it impact me, but I have repeated it over and over to people around me.

My action or reaction to any given situation does make all the difference. There are so many things in our lives over which we have no control. Just a few of the things Al and I have faced are the loss of three babies, Al's back surgery, my mother's battle with severe depression, job failures, loss of friendships, and finally, the loss of all of our parents.

How we have responded to each of these events in our lives has been the biggest test of our faith and our character. A big question for each of us is, "What do I do with something I don't like, I didn't ask for, I don't want, and I don't understand?" My action or reaction is my choice!

At the hard times in my life, I have often struggled trying to understand if this event was from God or from Satan. Most of those times I could not determine this clearly. I finally realized that more often than not, both God and Satan are involved (look at Job's life).

My part is to choose which direction this situation will take me—will it take me closer to God or pull me away from God. It is always Satan's will to take us totally away from God, but it is always God's will to bring us closer to him. It is up to me to make the right choice.

How I respond to any circumstance in my life is the vital issue.

7

Worry Is Like a
Rocking Chair

"...do not worry about your life."

Matthew 6:25

One of the greatest blessings of my life is the heritage of godly parents. My mom and dad were devoted to God, to each other, to my brother and me, to extended family and friends, and to people of all backgrounds regardless of age, nationality or economic status.

Mother died of leukemia in 1995; then Daddy was with my brother and sister-in-law and us till his death in 1998. The inheritance they left could not be measured in dollars; they were never rich by the world's standard. The lives they lived and the lessons they taught me are invaluable.

My dad had a special gift—an incredibly positive attitude toward life, whatever the circumstances. One of my greatest memories of him is his striding across the college campus where he taught Spanish and other foreign languages, whistling one of his favorite tunes! He would stop his whistling long enough to greet anyone who passed him.

Looking back, I know that his positive attitude was more than that; it was his deep faith in God that sustained his life. My dad's faith was evidenced by his choosing not to worry.

I will never forget an experience that he used to teach me a very important lesson. The summer before Al and I married, Al worked as a Bible salesman in Dallas, Texas. My home was in Abilene, Texas, about a three-hour drive west from Dallas. On some weekends after he finished with his work, Al would drive to Abilene to see me.

One of those week-ends I was waiting for his arrival. It got later and later; I went to the window at every sound of a car.

And with each trip to the window, I got more and more upset. My mind went from one bad scene to the next. I envisioned a car wreck with Al thrown on the highway!

Needless to say, with that kind of imagination, I was the "wreck" emotionally by the time Al arrived safe and sound. Remember, in the "old days" we didn't have cell phones, so it wasn't as easy as it is today to keep in close touch. After Al consoled me, he went on to his friend's house, and I went to bed exhausted from needless tears.

The next morning I replayed the night's scenario to my mom and dad. When I got to the frantic tears part, Daddy said, "Gloria, that is the craziest thing I've ever heard! If Al had been in an accident, you would have been in such a state that we would have to take care of you, and you would not be able to help Al. As it turned out, all your tears and worries were for nothing!"

His words still ring in my ears as I remember that night. All my emotionalism did no good—only damage. I would like to say I have never worried since that time, but to my shame, there have been too many times when anxiety has controlled me. Both that lesson and Daddy's own example have strengthened my convictions so that I have experienced more and more victories over worry.

One of Daddy's favorite sayings that I have often quoted is "Worry is like a rocking chair—it gives you something to do, but it doesn't get you anywhere." At least a rocking chair can give some comfort; worry certainly does not!

The apostle Paul in Philippians 4:6–7 gives us the antidote to worry:

> Do not be anxious about anything, but in everything, by prayer and petition, with thanksgiving, present your requests to God. And the peace of God, which transcends all understanding, will guard your hearts and your minds in Christ Jesus.

One of the statements I have made in describing my dad is that he was one of the most thankful persons I have ever known. Isn't it interesting that he was not a worrier? I am so grateful for a real-life display of the truth of this Biblical principle in the life of my dad. And I want to be the same example to my children and grandchildren.

8

Fight for Friendship

"...but there is a friend who sticks closer than a brother."

Proverbs 18:24b

Deep friendships don't just happen. They take time and work. Sometimes we even have to fight for the relationship to become what we want a true friendship to be.

Recently, I was reminded of this. A group of women were sharing some of their struggles and victories. Two of them described the changes in their relationship. For several years they had worked in the ministry together. Their husbands had leadership roles in the church, so the two couples often worked side by side.

In general, the people around them thought they were

great friends and even expected them to be. Each of the women, however, knew there was something missing. As they occasionally tried to address their individual concerns, their differences became more pronounced. They would retreat, assuming they would have to settle for just a superficial relationship.

This went on for several years with others occasionally trying to help them get a better understanding of each other. The relationship would improve to some degree, but past disappointments kept them from being vulnerable with one another.

Eventually God blessed their perseverance and helped each of these women to change and grow. As each of them got a clearer view of her own responsibility in the relationship, they began to trust each other more. With a growing trust they could be vulnerable and real, learning to value their different perspectives. Through humility and perseverance God gave them a great victory—the deep friendship they both desired!

One of the best-known examples of friendship in the Bible is the bond between David and Jonathan. There are many great qualities that marked their friendship—loyalty, trust, unselfishness, love and devotion.

As I study their relationship there is an aspect of it that continues to inspire me. At a time when Jonathan's father, King Saul, was searching for David to kill him, we read, "And Saul's son Jonathan went to David at Horesh and helped him find strength in God" (1 Samuel 23:16). The strength of their relationship was found in making God their strength.

Then later David was alone and was facing one of his greatest challenges. He had returned to his town to find it burned by the Amalekites. They had taken all the women and children captive, including David's two wives, and his own men were talking of stoning him. We are told in 1 Samuel 30:6 that "David found strength in the Lord his God."

We can surmise that David's friendship with Jonathan made a difference when they were apart and in distressing circumstances. The strongest and most lasting friendships must be grounded in a mutual dependence on God.

A recent email I received from one of my dearest friends gives me hope that this quality is in my friendships to some degree. In her memories of our friendship she shared,

> It was a time of big discoveries about God, about ourselves, about growing in a church.... We had long telephone talks discussing who we were, who He was, what we were supposed to do and to be and how in the world could we do it.

It was our sharing on a deep spiritual level, learning to find strength in the Lord that bonded us. Now that we are apart, each of us is stronger because of that aspect of our friendship.

Jesus gave the ultimate definition of true friendship in some of his last words to his closest disciples. He told them,

> "I no longer call you servants, because a servant does not know his master's business. Instead, I have called you friends, for everything that I learned from my Father I have made known to you." (John 15:15)

Having an intimate relationship with God and sharing that with others determines true Biblical friendship. There can be many kinds of friendship on many different levels, but no friendship will last into eternity without God and Jesus at the foundation.

The greatest victories come after the fiercest battles! Fighting the spiritual battle for our friendships calls for warriors, not wimps! In their book *Captivating*, John and Stasi Eldredge give a great description of women warriors:

> Women warriors are strong, yes, and they are also tender. There is mercy in them. There is vulnerability. In fact, offering a tender vulnerability can only

be done by an incredibly strong woman, a woman
rooted in Christ Jesus who knows *whose* she is and
therefore knows *who* she is.[1]

We face no greater enemy than Satan, who loves to
divide! We must hold on to our friendships, drawing on
God's power to continue to strengthen us together to win
his ultimate victory!

1. John and Stacy Eldredge, *Captivating* (Nashville: Thomas Nelson, 2005), 199.

9

❧

My Times Are in Your Hands

❧

"But I trust in you, O LORD;
 I say, 'You are my God.'
My times are in your hands."

Psalm 31:14–15

What is it that makes us think we are in control? At times it seems to almost start at infancy! Some babies do control everyone around them. At the baby's first whimper, everyone jumps to pacify; when baby is sleeping, absolute silence must be maintained!

Have you ever seen a two year old who is in control? That is not a pretty sight! In some ways our upbringing has trained us to think that we are the "center of the universe" or that everything should revolve around "me."

In contrast, others have been so out of control because of various abuses, that in reaction they say, "No one will ever control me again!" A woman struggling with past abuse once told me that there was a place deep in her heart that was hers alone, and she would never let anyone there. That was "control" to her.

In reality there is little that we really can control. My life's experiences have made me acknowledge that truth. Al and I married while we were still in college. Then about a year later, I got pregnant (so much for control!). My pregnancy went well, but seven weeks before the baby was due, I went into labor (definitely out of my control). Due to breathing difficulties, our baby boy died three days after he was born. That loss has shaped our lives in many ways.

Unexpected, unwanted events happen; their timing is so unplanned. The only thing that we could control in that situation was how we responded to the events. At that time we learned a lot about God's comfort, as well as the comfort from family and friends.

We knew we wanted to have another baby as soon as possible. Thankfully, about a year later and after I had finished my degree, we had our first daughter, Staci, who was very healthy though she was born five weeks early. This was one of the beginning lessons in showing us that God's timing is often different from ours.

As we look at the history of our immediate family, we see that our "times" are in God's hands. We would have never chosen to lose twin girls born after Staci. In fact, I thought we had gone through our "time" of suffering when we lost our first son. God again showed us his comfort in our sadness, and later gave us great joy in the birth of our daughter, Kristi.

Then when our youngest daughter, Keri, was born she developed breathing problems. This signaled "loss" to me since each of the three babies we did lose had breathing difficulties. Here again, we were forced to see our inability to control what was happening.

I vividly remember the tearful struggle I had surrendering Keri's life to God, knowing we might lose her. I know God wanted me to trust him! Al and I will never forget the nurse's report of the miraculous change in Keri's condition as she was taken in an ambulance to another hospital for specialized care. Her "times" were in God's hands!

Through the years it has been so evident that God's timing is perfect. In both insignificant small things to grand life-shaping events, God has shown his care for us.

Acts 17:26 reminds us that God cares for all of us:

> "...and he determined the times set for them and the exact places where they should live."

We have seen God's hand in determining the right husband at the right time for each of our girls. As their families have grown, we have been amazed at the timing of our grandbabies' births.

Staci and Andy were expecting the arrival of our first granddaughter when they were living in Milan, Italy. Al and I had planned a trip to the Middle East to help the churches there, and we hoped to be able to be in Milan close to the time of her birth. In our experience, it is difficult to predict the arrival of a baby, so we were in awe of God when we were able to be in Milan right after Kiara's birth and before she and Staci came home from the hospital—without having to adjust any of our tickets! That's God's timing!

Each of our precious grandbabies' births were timed by God. Even as Keri and Steve's first baby boy was stillborn, they were living close to us so that we were able to be with them and go through that hard time together. We helped each other hold on to God, trusting his control and timing.

After three daughters then six granddaughters, it was

God's timing that I was able to witness the birth of our first grandson, Brandon, Kristi and Greg's first baby.

As our parents aged, we entrusted them to God and his timing. There were times of sickness when we could be with them, and times when we were unable to go. When my mother was dying of leukemia, she seemed to hold on to life long enough to be able to see her first great-granddaughter, Kiara. I will forever be thankful for that special picture in my mind of their meeting.

Certainly one's birth and death—and all in between— are in God's hands. "All the days ordained for me were written in your book before one of them came to be" (Psalm 139:16). Being with my mom and three years later with my dad when they took their last breaths was a rich blessing to me. But whether I had been able to be with them or not, whatever the circumstances, we can be assured that our times are still in God's hands.

The rest of my life I want to put my trust in God. I am glad God is in control, not me!

10

Life Is So Daily

"Each day has enough trouble of its own."
Matthew 6:34

"Life is so daily." It's funny how some things stick in your mind. I can still remember the setting when my dear friend Pat Gempel made this statement about life. We had taken a trip to meet with another Christian sister. Pat and I were sharing with each other our personal concerns and struggles before we prayed together. Realizing that we both were feeling "heavy" with the varied situations we were facing, Pat sighed and said, "Life is so...daily!" We both laughed at the simple reality of that statement, and it has been a favorite saying of ours ever since.

Jesus' words in Matthew 6:34, "Each day has enough

trouble of its own," should help us avoid trying to take on a week or month or year all at once. Generally when I am feeling burdened and anxious, I am jumping ahead to things in the future. It is no wonder that I can quickly feel overwhelmed when I do this.

There is a principle in the Old Testament that helps me deal with the "daily-ness" of life. I call it the "manna principle." When the children of Israel were wandering in the desert for forty years, God provided bread from heaven, manna, for them. In Exodus 16:4 the Lord said to Moses,

> "I will rain down bread from heaven for you. The people are to go out each day and gather enough for that day. In this way I will test them and see whether they will follow my instructions."

Today we don't have the physical manna as they did, but we have spiritual manna—God's bread of life, his word—that is to feed and strengthen us. As each one gathered the physical manna each day, so each of us is responsible for gathering God's spiritual food daily. It does not work for me to have one good time in God's word to last for an entire week. I must go to God daily to have the strength for today.

God intends to provide exactly what I need for the challenges and circumstances he has planned on any given day. In a real sense, he is testing us to see if we will follow his instructions to rely on him in his way.

Each day does have enough trouble of its own, but with our God, each day also has enough strength of its own.

11

A Smile Goes
a Long Way

A cheerful look brings joy to the heart.

Proverbs 15:30

One of our yearly family traditions is to take a group picture of us, our three daughters, their husbands and our eight grandchildren. Have you ever tried to get sixteen people all looking at the camera with their eyes open—and smiling? The Baird family has found that to be quite an adventure.

Several years in a row there would be one grandchild who would not want to cooperate. It was never the same grandchild. It might be due to sickness, exhaustion or just plain "orneryness," but it affected the whole process. It was amazing to see what efforts all the rest of us made to try to get that one child to smile!

As the grandchildren have gotten older, it is easier to get smiles from everyone. Now we have to work on "real" smiles as some of the grandkids want to put the fake, Cheshire cat smile across their faces. We are not satisfied with the picture until we get a genuine smile from each one.

As simple as a smile is, it is a powerful thing. The effects of a smile are far reaching. A smile is contagious. Have you noticed that when you smile at someone, usually that person smiles back? A smile is one thing you can give away and keep at the same time.

A smile communicates warmth, friendliness and receptivity. A smile doesn't cost anything, but is extremely valuable. You can smile in any language thus crossing barriers of race and culture. Smiles are ageless, though the teeth—or lack thereof— may give clues to the age.

It would be hard to imagine a more precious smile than the first smile of a baby.

A smile can make someone's day. Smiles generate business—help make more sales, get better tips. In a recent discussion about customer service and the lack of it, my friend Patricia shared a time in her office when she taped a mirror on the phones of the sales people so that they could see their facial expressions as they talked to the customers. She wanted a pleasant look—a smile on their faces because it affected positively the way they talked.

Smiling is good for your health. Studies have shown that through the triggering of certain hormones, a smile promotes overall good health, leading to lower heart rate and steady breathing. A frown takes more muscles and effort and induces stress; in contrast a smile is a stress reliever, taking fewer muscles and less effort.

If smiles are so great, why don't we smile more? Some might say, "Look at the news! There isn't much to smile about!" Circumstances certainly affect us. There are tragedies around us daily—some we only hear about, but others hit us personally.

Yet even in the midst of hard times, a smile goes a long way. The wise man, Solomon, wrote in Proverbs 15:30, "A cheerful look brings joy to the heart." A smile can affect your feelings, warm your heart and lighten your load.

Solomon also wrote in the same chapter, verse 13, "A happy heart makes the face cheerful." When you feel good, your face will usually show it. Those verses have led me to say, "Smile when you feel like it, and when you don't feel like it—smile!" That seems like a good not-so-vicious cycle to adopt.

Dale Carnegie in his book, *How to Win Friends and Influence People*, said this about a smile:

> It costs nothing, but creates much. It enriches those who receive without impoverishing those who give. It happens in a flash and the memory of it sometimes lasts forever.[1]

Try smiling more! It is pretty cheap medicine—it will "make" your day and, very possibly, the day of someone else.

And your family pictures will look great!

---

1. Dale Carnegie, *How to Win Friends and Influence People* (New York: Simon and Shuster, original printing 1936), 76

12

※

Lessons from a Fall

※

The eye cannot say to the hand, "I don't need you!"

1 Corinthians 12:21

Treadmills can be dangerous! I have just had a serious encounter with one. Al and I have been faithfully exercising at the gym three times a week. On this fateful Monday morning, I stepped on the treadmill as usual, but unusually, it started moving before I had even programmed it. Needless to say, I wasn't prepared for that and did a three-point landing on my knees and mouth! Not a pretty sight!

As the people around me helped me get on my feet, I realized my lip was bleeding and my knees hurt. Only after I checked those injuries did I realize that my left hand was hurt. After a night with little sleep, Al took me to the emergency room for X-rays.

Fortunately, my hand was not broken; it was just soft tissue injuries. The doctor put a soft cast on my hand and forearm and sent me home with my arm in a sling. I counted my blessings that it wasn't broken and that it was my left hand since I am right-handed.

During the next few days, I learned several lessons. Since this was my first experience being in a cast, I began to realize firsthand what so many people have to cope with on a much bigger scale.

I thought of my friend, Robbie, who has had multiple surgeries to repair a knee injury, and is presently in a fixator—an apparatus on the outside of her leg that was surgically screwed inside her leg in order to hold it in place! It made my cast seem like nothing. In comparison to my injury, Robbie was challenged with pain multiplied—movement much more restricted—longer recuperation—need for getting help from others—greater temptation to be inwardly focused. Robbie has faced her challenges heroically by relying on God for her strength.

One morning as I was drying dishes with one hand, I marveled at the way God made us—two hands and two arms rather than one. It seems true that we don't really appreciate what we have until it is taken away from us.

For the most part, I so easily move about my day with no awareness of how my body parts are working together. It only takes an eyelash in my eye or a stubbed toe to get my attention, yet even then, I move on quickly taking the miraculous body for granted.

With my injured hand I had difficulty opening a jar or even pulling apart a zip-lock bag. I compensated by holding the jar between my arm and side. I used my teeth to pull on one side of the zip-lock bag! The obvious lesson is the unique value of each part of the body—even the smallest parts. This was a great reminder to me of God's comparing his body, the church, with the physical body.

Each person in the body of Christ is essential to the healthy functioning of the church. When each part is doing its work the way God intended, needs are met, growth occurs and God is glorified. When some parts are not working, it puts a strain on the rest of the body having to compensate for what others are not doing.

The first couple of days after my fall I was painfully aware of my hand. It throbbed and ached, making it difficult to position it comfortably. With the help of the cast and some Ibuprofen, the pain subsided.

It was interesting to me that after the major pain was dealt with, I became aware of the "little" injuries—my cut lip and my skinned knees stung with every movement.

While these were relatively insignificant hurts in the overall picture, they have been the longer term distraction. In thinking how we view "big" and "little" things, I reflected on dealing with sin in the process of becoming a Christian.

Usually we are aware of the more obvious sins such as immorality, hatred or lying. Even though these sins are difficult to work through, we usually focus first on repenting of these "big" ones. Then we may start feeling the pain of the "little" not-so-obvious things that have to change, such as insecurity or laziness. It may take more time to rid ourselves of these habits than some of the more obvious sins.

God does not see "big" sins and "little" sins in the way that we do. He has the answer for our injuries, big and little—Jesus, the great physician, who heals us physically, and more importantly, makes us whole spiritually.

It's amazing what you can learn from a bout with a treadmill!

13

Dealing with Temptation

"Why do you entertain evil thoughts in your hearts?"

Matthew 9:4b

We are having our neighbors over for coffee and dessert tomorrow night. I have gone to the grocery store to get fruit, cheese and crackers; I have made the pudding for a parfait dessert. There are fresh flowers on the table. Tomorrow I will be sure the house is clean. Then just before they come I will light the candles for a warm atmosphere. We might even light a fire in the fireplace if there is a chill in the air. We want everything to be ready to entertain our guests.

Entertaining is one of the most enjoyable aspects of homemaking for many of us women. We read magazines to get decorating ideas; we watch cooking shows for new recipes; we learn how to arrange flowers; we plan parties with different themes.

It takes a lot of time and effort to entertain. Since entertaining is such a pleasant experience for me, Jesus' question to the teachers of the law in Matthew 9:4 made me stop and reflect: "Why do you entertain evil thoughts"? That doesn't sound so pleasant, but isn't that what we often do?

The heart is really "Entertainment Central" for us. Jesus said in Matthew 15:19, "For out of the heart come evil thoughts, murder, adultery, sexual immorality, theft, false testimony, slander." The heart is like my home. I can prepare a godly atmosphere or I can let clutter and filth take over.

As I have to choose how to entertain my guests, I have to choose how I will entertain the thoughts and temptations that come my way.

Satan is the tempter. He often shoots his "flaming arrows" (Ephesians 6:16) in the form of a fleeting hateful or sexual thought, making us feel guilty. There have been times when some evil thought would suddenly come to my mind, without any prompting on my part, not from something I was reading or watching on TV—just like a "flaming arrow."

It has been so helpful for me to consider whether I am "entertaining" that thought or not. Just as I cannot determine who will ring our doorbell, I cannot always determine what temptation may spring into my mind. I can look through the peephole in the door to see who is ringing the bell. I can decide to open the door or not. I can open the door slightly, but not ask the person to come in.

If I do open the door and ask the person in, I can choose whether to ask him to sit down, or have a cup of tea, or stay for dinner…or move in with us!

So it is with our temptations. We have the choice to deal with them at early stages. We would be wise to have a clear peephole to check our thoughts. We need to be open quickly with others in revealing our temptations at early stages, so that we will have help in identifying the dangers that are lurking outside our door. We don't have to invite those evil thoughts in and "entertain" them.

By putting on God's armor and relying on others, we can have the victory God intends.

14

Counseling Myself

And I'll say to myself, "You have plenty of good
things laid up for many years. Take life easy;
eat, drink and be merry."

Luke 12:19

"Al doesn't know me as well as I know myself!" "He
thinks I can do this, but I'm not as smart as he is." "I can't
do what he thinks I can do."

These thoughts were flying through my mind as I was
wrestling with some challenge. I do not even remember
what the specifics were since it was a number of years
ago, but I do remember exactly where I was and the negative thoughts that were there.

I also remember that it alarmed me when I realized I

was trusting myself more than other people in my life. It's not that I don't need to have a mind of my own and to know what I think and feel about all kinds of things. No one can do my thinking for me. However, it can be dangerous to counsel myself. I have noticed that I can get very confused when I keep my thoughts completely to myself.

It is difficult to be objective about my own thoughts. Sometimes we can think too highly of our own thoughts, trusting ourselves more than anyone else. At other times we think so negatively that we do not give ourselves a chance to grow.

The Bible has many examples of people counseling themselves. Here are a few to consider:

Abraham (Genesis 20:11–12a):

> "I said to myself, 'There is surely no fear of God in this place, and they will kill me because of my wife.' Besides, she really is my sister."

This thinking nearly cost King Abimelech his life when he took Abraham's wife, Sarah, to be with him!

The Israelites (Deuteronomy 7:17):

> You may say to yourselves, "These nations are

> stronger than we are. How can we drive them out?"

Counseling themselves in this way made the Israelites fearful and faithless.

The Israelites again (Deuteronomy 8:17):

> You may say to yourselves, "My power and the strength of my hands have produced this wealth for me."

These are the arrogant self-sufficient thoughts that take the credit that belongs to God!

Moses about some people's attitude about God's covenant (Deuteronomy 29:19):

> He invokes a blessing on himself and therefore thinks, "I will be safe, even though I persist in going my own way."

This rebellious thinking will bring disaster.

The parable of the rich fool (Luke 12:16-21):

> v17—"He thought to himself, 'What shall I do? I have no place to store my crops.'"

v18—"Then he said, 'This is what I'll do. I will tear down my barns and build bigger ones...'"

v19—"And I'll say to myself, 'You have plenty of good things laid up for many years. Take life easy; eat, drink and be merry.'"

Look at God's answer to the rich man:

v20—"But God said to him, 'You fool! This very night your life will be demanded from you. Then who will get what you have prepared for yourself?'"

These examples should make us think carefully about what we think. The most difficult aspect of our trusting the thoughts that we are keeping in our own heads is that Satan loves to get in them!

Remember Jesus' description of Satan in John 8:44: Satan is "a liar and the father of lies." Remember how Satan deceived Eve: "Did God really say...?" and "You will not surely die" (Genesis 3:1, 4).

Satan is so crafty that he can make us think we are thinking our own thoughts. We need help in discerning what is true and what is Satan's lie.

Getting our thoughts in the light by saying them

aloud to others will help clarify the truth, especially as you compare your thoughts to God's thinking in his word.

15

❀

Boundaries

❀

I run in the path of your commands,
for you have set my heart free.

Psalm 119:32

On the last day of school, kids run out the school
door, flinging their arms in the air, shouting, "Free! We're
free!" A two-year-old after struggling in the confines of his
mother's arms will feel freed when she releases him to run
on the playground.

Freedom can mean the absence of rules, controls or
boundaries. However, this is not the meaning of true freedom in every case. A train is designed to run on a system
of tracks. When it stays on the tracks, it can go full steam
ahead! What happens if a train runs off the tracks? It is

out of control; it is wrecked. We can use those same words to describe a two-year-old without any boundaries! Boundaries are needed for our good.

God is the originator of boundaries. At creation he separated light from darkness and the water from dry land. Job describes this in Job 26:10: "He marks out the horizon on the face of the waters for a *boundary* between light and darkness" (emphasis mine).

God set a boundary in the Garden of Eden with Adam and Eve. He said to Adam,

> "You are free to eat from any tree in the garden; but you must not eat from the tree of the knowledge of good and evil, for when you eat of it you will surely die." (Genesis 2:16–17)

We know how Satan twisted Eve's thinking. The result of their sin created another boundary—this time they were not free to be in the garden; they were banished from it!

In recent years much has been written about boundaries. For me personally I have learned some important lessons through these books. When you work with other people, trying to help them through the issues in their lives, you can easily get "hooked in" to their ups and downs. I found that my feelings and moods would often be affected by how someone else was doing.

At other times Al and I would be held responsible for the health of another couple's marriage; if they weren't doing well, I would feel burdened. About this same time, we began working with the Chemical Recovery ministry which dealt with people having various addictions. We learned about co-dependency, which affects those around the addict.

The most helpful lesson about boundaries that I learned was that God has set boundaries for each individual—there are aspects of my life for which I have the sole responsibility. This is true for each one of us, and each of us will have to answer to God for those things.

In Chemical Recovery an expression used is "Sweep your side of the street." I am responsible for my health, physical appearance, attitudes, feelings, behavior, thoughts, abilities, desires, choices, words, reactions, etc. That should keep me busy!

One of my friends shared that her problem was she often took on someone else's responsibilities and failed to accept her own responsibilities! This might be more common than we would like to admit. Of course, we must care about others and help them in any way we can. But we cannot change someone else; we cannot make someone else repent.

Teaching individual responsibility to our children is essential to their maturity. It helps to realize that there are many adults who have not matured in this way. The best way we can assist others is to help them understand God's boundaries. Helping them find God's track will give them freedom.

When we stay on the path of God's commands, we can run! We are truly free! We can say with David,

> The boundary lines have fallen for me in
>   pleasant places;
>   surely I have a delightful inheritance.
>   (Psalm 16:6)

16

Spiritual Glasses

"Your eye is the lamp of your body. When your eyes are good, your whole body also is full of light. But when they are bad, your body also is full of darkness."

Luke 11:34

When I was young, I had a remarkable piano teacher. She was blind, but this did not keep her from being an excellent pianist. She would put her hands over my hands as I played so that she could "see" how I positioned my fingers.

As a whole, her family was even more amazing. For years she and her two brothers, who were also blind, lived in a home on their own. It was disconcerting to neighbors and friends who would drive by their dark house at night.

Of course, they did not need the lights!

All three were gifted musicians—she was the pianist, another brother sang beautifully and directed a college choir, and the other brother played the cello. At one point they had a music group called "The Three Blind Mice"! They did their own cooking, did woodwork with power tools, operated a recording studio and more. Their physical limitations did not seem to limit them.

Seeing is really about perspective. In John 9:39, after Jesus had given sight to the man born blind, he said, "For judgment I have come into this world, so that the blind will see and those who see will become blind."

The "sighted" Pharisees were indignant when they realized Jesus was calling them blind. To them Jesus said, "If you were blind, you would not be guilty of sin; but now that you claim you can see, your guilt remains" (v41).

Jesus was talking about much more than physical sight. The way we see things makes all the difference. The proverbial "glass half full" or the "glass half empty" exemplifies perspective. How we view the hard things in our lives (and even the not-so-hard things) can make or break us depending on how we see them.

It is important to recognize that our family background, our personalities, our cultural influences and our experiences are some of the shaping influences of our perspectives. Books such as *Adult Children of Alcoholic Parents* and *What Children Learn from Their Parents' Marriage* highlight these influences.[1]

It helps to realize that each person will look at a situation through his or her unique glasses. Dealing with loss is often a time when differences of perspective will surface. Since Al and I have shared losses of our babies and later on, the losses of our parents, we have learned that we handle our grief differently. There is no right and wrong when it comes to grieving, but not everyone realizes that.

We get into trouble when we expect someone "to get over it" on our timetable. When we as friends share more of our backgrounds with each other and learn to appreciate our differences, we will be more able to sensitively support one another through the hard times.

When we become Christians, our eyes are opened. We can say with the blind man in John 9, "Once I was blind, now I see." Our perspective changes; we put on our spiritual glasses. In 2 Corinthians 5:16 Paul said, "So from now on we regard no one from a worldly point of view."

The problem is we can be quick to take off those spiritual glasses, replacing them with our more comfortable "this is the way I am" glasses.

1. Janet Woititz, *Adult Children of Alcoholic Parents* (Deerfield Beach, FL: HCI, 1990).

Judith P. Siegel, *What Children Learn from Their Parents' Marriage* (New York: Harper Paperback, 2001).

Negativity, hopelessness, complaining, criticalness—these are signs that we are wearing the old glasses. When we look through the glasses of God's word, we see clearly; we have the 20/20 vision that only truth can bring. We have to continually search to find God's perspective. Only then will we truly see.

17

Live Until You Die

"I have come that they may have life, and have it to the full."

John 10:10b

Driving to worship on Sunday morning, I turned to Al and said, "I love how Lin lives life!"

My friend Lin was in Los Angeles to speak at a Women's Day (actually two—one in English and one in Spanish). She brought her pre-teen daughter and a teen friend with her because she wanted to show them some of her favorite places in Laguna Beach and in LA, but also wanted them to be able to meet other girls their ages.

Those opportunities were provided through a beach devotional with teen girls in San Diego, then a late night small group time with mothers and daughters.

In the midst of all this, Lin was reconnecting with many dear friends, having deep spiritual talks, seeking advice for her life, yet shopping, and even seeing the musical, *Wicked*. What a full weekend!

Lin lives life fully. When she works, she gives her all; when she plays, she enjoys it totally. She laughs loudly; she cries unashamedly. When she gives, she gives wholeheartedly; she values deeply what she receives from others. Lin would be the first to share her imperfections with you. She is not a superwoman, only a woman who considers God her best friend, knowing her absolute need for him.

Lin is a woman who has seen more of death up close and personal than most people. Maybe that is why she squeezes all the good she can out of a day.

She used her vocation as a nurse in a way she would never have planned: she nursed her husband, Barry, through years of battling an unusual type of brain cancer until he died seven years ago.

In the next few years she lost a brother with the same cancer that had taken Barry's life, then her dad died, and most recently, she lost another brother. In all, she has suffered the loss of nine close friends and family members in the last seven years! At this time Lin is working in a children's hospital in the cancer ward! Death has pushed Lin to value every moment in life.

One of my favorite country and Western songs is Tim McGraw's "Live Like You Were Dying." The song is about a man dealing with the news of his life ending soon. The chorus is his response to the question, "How's it hit 'cha when you get that kind of news?"

> Chorus:
> I went skydiving
> I went rocky mountain climbing
> I went two point seven seconds on a bull named
>   Fu Man Chu
> And I loved deeper
> And I spoke sweeter
> And I gave forgiveness I'd been denyin'
> And he said some day I hope you get the chance
> To live like you were dyin'[2]

In reality we are all in the process of dying even though we live like we have many more years ahead of us. Today is all we have! Yesterday is past, and tomorrow is future. The quality of our lives would be much richer if we really made the most of each day.

Instead we seem to either regret the past or relive the "good old days." As for the future, too often we think our

2. Tim J. Nichols, Craig Michael Wiseman, "Live Like You Were Dying," recorded by Tim McGraw.

enjoyment is yet to come, or we are fearful about what might happen tomorrow.

In Matthew 6:34 Jesus told us not to worry about tomorrow. He emphasized the importance of living today by reminding us that "each day has enough trouble of its own." One of the richest blessings Jesus intends for us to enjoy is to have life to the full (John 10:10b). This is possible by doing it his way—one day at a time!

18

Why Am I Here?

> "Even the stork in the sky knows her appointed seasons."
>
> Jeremiah 8:7

You can meet some interesting people when you travel. Al tells about a woman seated next to him on a flight from Boston to London. She was an oceanographer returning to London after a trip to South America on an assignment.

She was to do her regular BBC telecast on oceanography, then she was off to ski in the Alps. In the summer she raced cars! Not exactly your ordinary run-of-the-mill lifestyle.

At one point in their conversation, Al asked her what

she would say her purpose in life was. She paused in thought and said, "That's a good question—I'm really not sure."

Similarly, a well-known star pro quarterback was asked the same question in an interview. He seemed "stumped" or at least caught off-guard by it and never really gave an answer.

If you look around a room, everything in it has a purpose, even if the item is just for decorative appeal. When we do see an unfamiliar object, we usually ask, "What is this for?"

Doesn't it seem strange that men and women, God's greatest creation, have such a difficult time understanding why we are here? The prophet Jeremiah addressed God's people,

> "Even the stork in the sky
>   knows her appointed seasons,
> and the dove, the swift and the thrush
>   observe the time of their migration.
> But my people do not know
>   the requirements of the LORD." (Jeremiah 8:7)

Maybe it has to do with not reading the instruction manual!

There was a period of time several years ago when our dishwasher was broken. I found that it actually made a good dish drain. I could wash and rinse the dishes then put them in the racks of the dishwasher to dry. If someone had watched me do this not knowing the dishwasher was broken, she would have thought I was crazy for doing that extra work when the dishwasher was made for that purpose. Certainly, it could be used as a dish drain, but how foolish it would be to not use it as the designer intended.

The one who makes an object is the one who knows why it was made and how it is to be used. So it is with God! He is our creator; he knows how we will function best and he hasn't left us in the dark. His word is our instruction manual. Only as we look to him will we find real purpose and meaning in our lives. Here are some meaningful instructions to help us know why we are here:

> Matthew 22:37–39: "Jesus replied: 'Love the Lord your God with all your heart and with all your soul and with all your mind.' This is the first and greatest commandment. And the second is like it: 'Love your neighbor as yourself.'"

> 1 Corinthians 10:31: So whether you eat or drink or whatever you do, do it all for the glory of God.

> 2 Corinthians 5:9: So we make it our goal to

please him, whether we are at home in the body or away from it.

2 Corinthians 5:20: We are therefore Christ's ambassadors, as though God were making his appeal through us. We implore you on Christ's behalf: Be reconciled to God.

Thankfully, God has left us instructions to give direction and meaning to our lives. We don't have to foolishly go through life wondering what it is all about; nor do we have to pursue every possible course in order to find fulfillment. Our Creator's way works!

19

Stones of Remembrance

"In the future, when your children ask you, 'What do these stones mean?' tell them that the flow of the Jordan was cut off before the ark of the covenant of the LORD. When it crossed the Jordan, the waters of the Jordan were cut off. These stones are to be a memorial to the people of Israel forever."

Joshua 4:6–7

The older I get, the more I appreciate any helps that jog my memory. I have notes all around me, reminding me of phone calls to make, appointments to keep and groceries to buy. I have joked that I just need to remember where the notes are!

It helps my feelings when someone much younger

than I am forgets someone's name too. Forgetfulness is not just an old-age malady.

Today's events quickly crowd out yesterday's happenings. In fact, our "todays" are so full that we can easily forget what happened this morning.

There are some things we should never forget. In the marriage classes we teach, Al frequently tells the husbands that there are dates they should never forget: your wife's birthday, your anniversary, Valentine's Day and Mother's Day.

God continually put reminders for us throughout his word. To remind Adam and Eve (and us) of their sin, God told Adam that he would have to work the cursed ground through painful toil. He told Eve that her pain in childbearing would greatly increase.

After the flood God set the rainbow in the clouds as a reminder that he would never again destroy the earth with a flood.

Through the time of the patriarchs, pillars would often be set up to remember experiences with God.

With Moses and the Israelites God instructed the keeping of the Passover to remind them of his delivering them out of Egypt.

God gave Joshua very specific instructions to bring stones from the Jordan River to be a memorial to the

Israelites of his miraculously leading them across the river at flood stage!

These twelve stones were to serve as a sign among the Israelites, but God also cared about the future generations. He wanted their children to know and remember the powerful ways he had worked to save his people.

Psalm 78 is almost a history lesson of God and his people, but more than that, it is a wake-up call urging us to remember what God has done. The psalmist shows clearly how God wants his commands passed on to the future generations, and also conveys strongly how God feels about his people forgetting his great deeds.

> I will open my mouth in parables,
>   I will utter hidden things, things from of old—
> what we have heard and known,
>   what our fathers have told us.
> We will not hide them from their children;
>   we will tell the next generation
> the praiseworthy deeds of the LORD,
>   his power, and the wonders he has done.
> He decreed statutes for Jacob
>   and established the law in Israel,
> which he commanded our forefathers
>   to teach their children,
> so the next generation would know them,
>   even the children yet to be born,
>   and they in turn would tell their children.

> Then they would put their trust in God
> > and would not forget his deeds
> > but would keep his commands.
> They would not be like their forefathers—
> > a stubborn and rebellious generation,
> whose hearts were not loyal to God,
> > whose spirits were not faithful to him.
> Psalm 78:2–8

The entire Psalm goes through the Israelites' times of remembering and times of forgetting. Verses 41–42 read,

> Again and again they put God to the test;
> > they vexed the Holy One of Israel.
> They did not remember his power—
> > the day he redeemed them from the
> > > oppressor.

We don't use the word "vexed" often, but it is frightening to think of irritating God! Hopefully, this underscores how important it is for us to remember what God has done in our lives.

What are your stones of remembrance? God's intent is for us to look back at the victories he has given so that our faith will be stronger as we face new challenges. Have you passed on to your children the great deeds God has accomplished in your life?

For me one of the biggest motivations for writing this book was to be sure that I share these life lessons with my children and grandchildren. Our faith today can make a difference for generations to come.

20

Lifelines

"The words I have spoken to you are spirit and they are life."

John 6:63b

Without sounding overly dramatic, I can honestly say that I think I would be in a mental institution or dead without God's word. On my own, my thinking can take me to some dark places. By nature, I am fearful, anxious and worried. I have seen with myself and others where negative, self-focused thinking can go if left unchecked. The only weapon that will cut through the lies of Satan is the truth, and the truth is the word of God.

Jesus claimed that his words are life (John 6:63). In the Old Testament Moses declared about the words of the law in Deuteronomy 32:47: "They are not just idle words for you—they are your life."

Through the years I have found passages in the Bible that have rescued me from spiritual "drowning." In much the same way that a person drowning in the ocean needs a lifeline to pull them into the boat or to shore, I have needed God's lifelines from his word to draw me back to safety.

For me it has been important to write these lifelines in a journal or on index cards that I can carry with me. Doing this has helped me to memorize the verses so that I can repeat them to myself during times of temptation or weakness. In this way my thoughts can be "reprogrammed" with God's truth.

Here are some lifelines that are helpful to me:

Romans 8:28

> And we know that in all things God works for the good of those who love him, who have been called according to his purpose.

When things are happening that I don't understand or don't want to happen, it helps me to remember this promise of God.

Romans 8:1

> Therefore, there is now no condemnation for those who are in Christ Jesus.

My accused nature can pull me down; this verse encourages me.

Proverbs 3:5-7

> Trust in the LORD with all your heart
>   and lean not on your own understanding;
> in all your ways acknowledge him,
>   and he will make your paths straight.
> Do not be wise in your own eyes;
>   fear the LORD and shun evil.

I don't have to know and understand everything. My part is to trust God and to stay on his path away from evil. God will do his part.

Psalm 16 (all of it, especially vv5–6)

> LORD, you have assigned me my portion and
>   my cup;
>   you have made my lot secure.
> The boundary lines have fallen for me in
>   pleasant places;
>   surely I have a delightful inheritance.

God is involved in my life; I can be secure because of him.

Psalm 18 (all of it, especially vv28–29)

> You, O LORD, keep my lamp burning;
>   my God turns my darkness into light.
> With your help I can advance against a troop;
>   with my God I can scale a wall.

When I am insecure, lacking confidence and saying, "I can't," these verses show me that with God I can. Verse 35 says, "You stoop down to make me great" This helps me know how much God loves me and cares about me!

Isaiah 43:2, 4

> "When you pass through the waters, I will be with you.... Since you are precious and honored in my sight, and because I love you."

God is with me in the hard times, and I am very special to him.

Each of us needs unique lifelines to deal with our own weaknesses and temptations. It is so faith building to find these strong ties to God in his word and to see the difference when we consistently put his word into practice in our lives.

There is not a day that goes by that we do not need God's word. It is our life!

21

Don't Waste Your Suffering

No discipline seems pleasant at the time, but painful. Later on, however, it produces a harvest of righteousness and peace for those who have been trained by it.

Hebrews 12:11

What do you do with hardship or with painful situations? Most of us just want the pain to go away. We try to explain it or understand it or even deny it. In our early marriage, Al and I lost our first baby, a son born seven weeks early. Our baby lived about three days, but when we lost him, I questioned God, begging to understand.

I remember asking, "Did we do something wrong? Are you punishing us? Why is this happening to us?" There are so many things that happen to us or around us that we cannot understand or explain. As I am writing this, a friend is agonizing over the sudden death of her thirty-two-year-old husband and being left as a widow with three young children. Who of us would not be asking, "Why?"

Humanly, we look for answers, and not infrequently, the answers we seek do not come. For us as Christians, we know that our God is all powerful, but we also know that Satan is a very real and powerful enemy. As I said earlier, I have struggled with trying to decide if a particular situation was from God or from Satan. I have accepted that God and Satan use the same circumstances, and it is up to us individually to choose which direction we will go in any given situation.

We can pull closer to God, to be more dependent on his word and his people, or pull away from him and convince ourselves that he doesn't really care about us. It is always God's will to pull us closer to him; it is always Satan's will to pull us away from God! It is our choice which way we go.

Years ago I heard it said, "You can waste your time, your energy, your money, but don't waste your suffering!"

That statement got my attention. It is frightening to think that I might actually prolong or repeat painful experiences by failing to learn from them.

In the midst of the pain of losing our baby, I could sense a difference in *asking* "why?" and in *demanding* "why?" The demanding attitude—the "tell me or else" quickly leads to bitterness, which pulls us away from God. The asking "why?" was a soul-wrenching cry for an answer, yet a willing surrender to a loving God whether or not the answer came.

Surrender brings comfort and peace and reinforces our trust in God. As we trust him, we begin to learn some of life's greatest lessons, even in our pain.

As I look back at my life, it seems that the deepest lessons I have learned and the greatest character changes I have made have come through difficult times. Whatever happens in my life, I want to draw closer to God knowing he gives me the ultimate victory. I don't want to waste my suffering!

22

Words, Words, Words

When words are many, sin is not absent,
but he who holds his tongue is wise.
Proverbs 10:19

A common complaint that wives have about their husbands is that they don't talk enough. When a wife mentions this to me, my usual response is, "Maybe if you talk less, he will talk more!"

I learned this firsthand with my own husband. Early in our marriage after we had been with another couple, I mentioned to Al that he had been quiet in the conversations. His reply was, "Gloria, you didn't give me a chance to say anything."

It was especially embarrassing to realize how unaware

I was of monopolizing the conversation. That was a beginning point for me personally to see that I needed help from others to change that bad habit. I decided that after being in situations like that, I needed to ask Al how I did in limiting my comments, giving others a chance to speak.

Learning to control my tongue is a life-long process. I am not alone in this challenge. In James 3:8 we read, "But no man can tame the tongue..." and in verse 2:

> We all stumble in many ways. If anyone is never at fault in what he says, he is a perfect man, able to keep his whole body in check.

As we all have experienced, our words can be helpful or they can be very damaging. We can build someone up, or we can tear someone down with a few words.

Al and I have called Ephesians 4:29 the "Golden Rule of Communication." It reads,

> Do not let any unwholesome talk come out of your mouths, but only what is helpful for building others up according to their needs, that it may benefit those who listen.

Not only do we have to take responsibility for our words said to another person, we also have to realize that anyone else who hears those words is affected by them as well. Whether we like it or not, we are responsible for what we say.

One of the most difficult challenges in life is knowing what to say and when to say it. I have already confessed that I am a woman of many words. So, what do I do with all these words? I need to talk to someone, don't I?

There are verses in two Psalms that have been very practical helps to me in this. First, Psalm 142:1–2:

> I cry aloud to the LORD;
> > I lift up my voice to the LORD for mercy.
> I pour out my complaint before him;
> > before him I tell my trouble.

God can handle my words! I can unload all of them on him; he isn't too tired or too busy to listen. My feelings, my hurts, my burdens, my joys, my sorrows—God hears them all.

As a parent, I can get a glimpse of God's eagerness to hear us. I wanted our girls to feel free to come to me, their mother, to express anything they were feeling. I wanted them to be open and real, yet respectful as they conveyed their concerns.

We can pour out our complaints to God, but we need to remember that he is God! Pouring out our hearts to

God without reservations or fears should release much of the pressure we feel. Then we are ready for the next step.

David said in Psalm 141:3,

> Set a guard over my mouth, O LORD;
>   keep watch over the door of my lips.

We need God's help to keep our words in check. I am not able to adequately determine when and what to speak. Asking God to keep watch for me and humbly seeking help from people around me is my best defense against harming others with my words.

Words are powerful! We need to be aware of how we use them. Jesus makes this very clear in Matthew 12:36–37:

> But I tell you that men will have to give account on the day of judgment for every careless word they have spoken. For by your words you will be acquitted, and by your words you will be condemned.

It is sobering to realize how seriously God takes the words we speak. This passage shows us how important it is to weigh our words carefully.

Before the talkative, "accused" ones of us get overwhelmed, I want to quickly remind us of God's grace! Our forgiveness starts and ends with grace. None of us deserves or could ever earn his grace. It is the gift of God (Ephesians 2:8). As much as I want to be perfect in my speech and judgment, I know I fail, and it helps me to consider such scriptures as these:

> If you, O LORD, kept a record of sins,
>   O LORD, who could stand?
> But with you there is forgiveness;
>   therefore you are feared. (Psalm 130:3–4)

> As far as the east is from the west,
>   so far has he removed our transgressions
>   from us. (Psalm 103:12)

When God forgives, he forgets. Rather than being overwhelmed, we can overflow with gratitude for the forgiveness of God, thankful that when we are humble and contrite, the blood of Jesus keeps on cleansing us as we continue to grow into his likeness.

As we consider our words, we can join the Psalmist David in his prayer in Psalm 19:14:

> May the words of my mouth
>   and the meditation of my heart
> be pleasing in your sight,
>   O LORD, my Rock and my Redeemer.

Our goal should always be for our words to be pleasing to God, and we should be seriously committed to this goal. However, if and when we fall short of our goal, we need to be humble and repentant, and we need to accept God's gracious forgiveness.

23

✤

Everything Is Against Me!

✤

Their father Jacob said to them, "You have deprived me of my children. Joseph is no more and Simeon is no more, and now you want to take Benjamin. Everything is against me!"

Genesis 42:36

In the movie *Parenthood*, there was a memorable scene for me as a mother. As Steve Martin (the dad) was looking at his teen-aged son, he had two drastically different "visions" of his son in the future. One was a scene of his son—a sniper shooting wildly into a crowd and screaming obscenities, blaming his dad for his horrible life. The other scene was his son at graduation giving a speech saying he owed his dad everything for all his help and support through the years.

While I laughed along with everyone else in the movie theater, I also realized how quickly I as a mother of three girls could switch from one extreme view to the other depending on the circumstances.

I remember one particular set of parent-teacher conferences. When we met with each of our girls' teachers, we got a similar report on each one. Basically, the girls were quite capable but they often went to the teacher to be assured they were doing an assignment correctly when they really knew enough to do the work without help.

I remember thinking we had ruined the girls for life— that somehow we hadn't given them the support they needed to be confident. Certainly, there were things we needed to learn to help them, but they were not ruined for life! (Now one of our greatest blessings is seeing our three daughters as strong Christian wives and mothers!)

This experience was just one of many situations with our girls in which I over-reacted. Somewhere in those times I began to realize what I was doing and reminded myself with, "Today is not the *whole* of my life" (or my kids' lives). That has been helpful to bring me back to reality, and I have often shared that thought with others.

A few years ago as I was reading the account of Joseph in Genesis, I was struck with Jacob dealing with a similar life-is-ruined mindset. After Joseph's brothers had gone to Egypt to get grain because of a severe famine, they returned to Jacob with grain, but without their brother, Simeon. Joseph, without identifying himself to his brothers, had insisted on keeping Simeon in prison in Egypt to test their honesty. He also made it clear that they were not to come back to Egypt without bringing Benjamin, their youngest brother.

When the brothers informed Jacob about all of this, he replied, "You have deprived me of my children. Joseph is no more and Simeon is no more, and now you want to take Benjamin. *Everything is against me!*" (Genesis 42:36, emphasis added).

At the time the facts as he knew them were true and real. Yet his "everything is against me" could not have been further from the truth. Because of God, the truth was that everything was *for* him. God was not only saving their lives from the famine, but was also about to restore his whole family to him—Joseph included. What a future God had in store for him! That day was definitely not the whole of Jacob's life though the facts and feelings seemed to prove otherwise.

When you are having one of those days, remember—with God, today is not the whole of your life! Only God has the whole picture.

24

Web or Net?

What he trusts in is fragile;
  what he relies on is a spider's web.

Job 8:14

On a walk down a beautiful nature trail, I stopped to look at a spider's web. I am intrigued at the intricacies of something so fragile. With one swipe I can destroy something that took the spider hours to spin, and yet, the web is strong enough to catch the spider's prey.

Have you ever watched a spider spin its web? There have been a few times I was able to see part of the process. It is fascinating to realize that a spider produces different kinds of silk to spin its web. One type is sticky and is used to catch its prey; another type is non-sticky and is stronger. The non-sticky silk is the part that the spider uses for the stronger "spokes of the wheel," and these are the ones he spins first to anchor the web.

Then the spider moves on the non-sticky threads, but it is possible for a spider, if startled, to get tangled in its own web.

The purpose of the web is to catch the spider's life-sustaining food—its prey will be eaten!

Compare a spider's web to a safety net. Though much bigger and stronger, a safety net has a similar configuration. It has the larger cables that give the net its main strength. Then there are smaller ropes interwoven to prevent an object from passing through the net. The purpose of a safety net is to prevent injury or even death.

An interesting consideration is to think about our relationships from the viewpoint of a spider's web or a safety net. Our relationships with other people tell a lot about us as individuals. Each of us has many people with whom we interact on a regular basis. Whether we realize it or not, those people influence us, and we influence them as well. The question to ask is what kind of influence is being exerted?

With our children we are concerned about the peer pressure they face. We know from our own experiences that there are times we did something we would not have done on our own; we simply went along with the crowd.

I remember a time when one of our girls, along with two of her friends, "bullied" a girl from another street. It is not that I think my daughter would not possibly do such a thing, but I do know the group influence is great.

In times like these, friendships can be like the spider's web. As an individual, I can think I am strong enough to have a good influence on my friends. But if I am not careful, like the spider, I can get caught in a web of relationships with the negative, worldly pull being greater than the positive, godly influence.

Paul's warning in 1 Corinthians 15:33 is good to remember: "Do not be misled: 'Bad company corrupts good character.'"

For our relationships to be like a safety net rather than a spider's web, we need to have deep convictions based on God's word. Character counts especially in our friendships. What we talk about, what we do, where we go, how we respond—these are all critical aspects that determine the quality of our relationships.

A safety-net connection should give support, encouragement, hope, vision to be our best, and loving challenge to change what needs to be changed. The power of influence is obvious in 1 Timothy 4:16:

> Watch your life and doctrine closely. Persevere
> in them, because if you do, you will save both
> yourself and your hearers.

This describes a real safety net.

The truth is our relationships can change from spider's web to safety net and back again due to the "ups and downs" in our lives. Again realizing that often God and Satan are at work in the same situations, it is vital that each of us takes responsibility to be the best friend we can be and to be sure we choose the company that will help us become more like Christ.

25

True Security

LORD, you have assigned me my portion and
my cup;
you have made my lot secure.

Psalm 16:5

When Al finished graduate school at the University of Texas, we moved to Burlington, Massachusetts, primarily to be a part of a church planting. He got a great job with the Sperry Research Center and loved working there for the next fifteen years.

The Research Center was located on forty acres of land, bordering White's Pond in Sudbury. The employees jokingly called it "Sperry Country Club" since they could swim, play tennis, jog, etc. in the beautiful surroundings on their lunch hour!

Al's working there for fifteen years gave us a sense of security. We had health benefits, vacation time, bonuses and a great retirement plan.

At this same time Bob and Pat Gempel invited us to breakfast. They had more than breakfast to offer us! They asked us to consider Al giving up his career for a new one—to become a full-time elder in the fast-growing, young Boston Church of Christ!

We went home with our heads spinning! It was really a dream offer to us because our hearts' desire had always been to serve God fully; it just seemed that Al's job provided the funds for our doing that. At that time the Boston Church was not able to provide the same kind of financial support that we had with Sperry. Certainly, at that time, there was no retirement plan.

Somewhere in this time of weighing out the pros and cons, I realized that my security was tied to our finances. We were very comfortable and really had no financial concerns. Before this time, I would have been sure that my security was in God! This opportunity was about more than finances; it challenged us in the basics of our trust in God.

Giving up Al's career was not the hardest part of making our decision. If we accepted the offer, it meant leaving the church family we had been part of for fifteen years.

The next weeks and months involved some of the deepest soul-searching, advice-seeking, list-making, prayer-and-fasting times of our lives.

Finally, convinced that this was God's offer, we made the decision to accept the full-time work with the Boston Church. When Al announced our plans at Sperry, he got some interesting responses. One guy said, "Oh, you are going from physics to metaphysics!"

Again, it was much easier to make the announcement at work, than it was to tell the dear friends at church that we were going to be working with another church family.

A month or so after we made our decision, Al came home from Sperry, saying, "Gloria, you will not believe what has happened at work!" The news was that the entire Research Center was closing! From top to bottom—each employee was without a job unless he chose to move to another state.

We were shocked—and in awe of God! Al already had his new job. Even his atheist co-workers were making comments pointing upward and asking Al if he wanted any disciples. We have called this miraculous event "God's exclamation point to our decision."

And my view of security? What a lesson to learn—what I thought was security was not security at all. Only with God is our lot really secure.

26

❧

Forgiveness, God's Freedom

❧

> Be kind and compassionate to one another, forgiving each other, just as in Christ God forgave you.
>
> Ephesians 4:32

Forgiveness is a godly action. It doesn't come naturally, and it isn't easy. Left to my own nature, my first impulse when people hurt me is to want to hurt them back. I want them to understand how they hurt me and to feel sorry that they hurt me. Then I might possibly be willing to forgive them—if they promise not to do it again! Can you identify with those feelings?

Years ago a friend of mine was desperately struggling to forgive her husband. He had left her for another woman, leaving her with their four children! The hurt was so deep! What a selfish, thoughtless action!

Didn't she have every right to demand justice? Not according to Jesus. He said,

> "For if you forgive men when they sin against you, your heavenly Father will also forgive you. But if you do not forgive men their sins, your Father will not forgive your sin." (Matthew 6:14–15)

Recognizing our own sins and our need for forgiveness helps move us toward forgiving others. Even though my friend acknowledged this, there was a part of her that felt her husband would get off "scot free" if she forgave him.

This was Satan's twist to keep her in his clutches! In reality her husband was going on with his life, while she was emotionally paralyzed by her anger and hatred.

The article from *None of These Diseases* on the next page describes her plight in very graphic terms.

How to Be a Slave

Hate somebody. The moment you start hating a man you become his slave. He controls your thoughts, invades your dreams, absorbs your creativity and determines your appetite. He affects your digestion, robs you of your peace of mind and good will and takes away the pleasure of your work. He ruins your religion, nullifies your prayers, and you can't enjoy your vacation anymore.

He destroys your freedom of mind, and he hounds you wherever you go. You cannot get away from the man you hate. He is with you when you wake up and invades your privacy when you eat. He is close beside you when you drive your car, affects your attitude on the job and distracts your mind so you can have neither efficiency nor happiness.

He influences even your tone of voice when you speak to your boss, your wife or your child. He requires you to take medicines for indigestion, headache, and loss of energy. He steals your last moments before you go to sleep. You want to be a slave? Find somebody and hate him.[1]

---

1. Adapted from *None of These Diseases* by S. I. McMillen (Grand Rapids: Fleming H. Revell, 1984).

The truth is that my forgiving someone frees me! It frees me from hatred, bitterness, resentment and other things that take away my joy. It frees me from letting another person and his actions control me. That person's sin is not cleared by my forgiveness, but by his own repentance and the blood of Christ. When I forgive others, it frees me to be forgiven by God.

No wonder Satan tries to get me to withhold forgiveness. Forgiveness is God's way to our freedom!

27

❦

Following Directions

❦

> Your word is a lamp to my feet
> and a light for my path.
>
> Psalm 119:105

Los Angeles is infamous for its traffic. It doesn't seem to matter what time of the day or night you are driving; the freeways can become a "parking lot" for no apparent reason.

When we first moved, driving was intimidating to me. We moved here from Boston, so I was accustomed to aggressive driving, but the sheer size of Los Angeles was the intimidating factor for me. One of the first essential gifts we were given was the *Thomas Guide*. We never drove anywhere in the LA area without it. It is one of the best street maps I have ever seen. With my trusty *Thomas Guide* I feel confident to tackle the streets of LA! I realize this dates me; now so many rely on their GPS. Even along with Google Maps, I still frequently use the *Thomas Guide*.

Knowing my need for the *Thomas Guide* to help me as I drive, I am amazed that people seem to think they should be able to find their way in life without a guide. This makes as much sense to me as it would to try to find my way to downtown LA from my house simply by going up and down each street I come to until some day I make it downtown!

It would be interesting to see what kind of directions I would give to someone else after that trip. Too often the advice people are quick to give may be based on their own "ups and downs" rather than solid truth.

With all the relational difficulties and complex problems in today's world, it is easier to tell someone what does not work rather than what does work.

When microwave ovens first came out, my mother did not want to use one. She would have had to learn a new way of cooking, using different pans. It wasn't worth that extra effort to her.

A person could try using a microwave without reading the manual that came with it. She might use one of her favorite metal pans in the microwave—and very soon, she would see sparks flying resulting in a ruined microwave! I have heard of eggs "exploding" and have personally hardened some bread by not following the instructions!

For any new appliance or gadget, it makes sense to read and follow the manufacturer's instructions. The manufacturer knows what the object was designed to do as well as how it will work the most efficiently.

Since God is our Creator and the Author of life itself, doesn't it make sense to go to him and to his "instruction manual," the Bible, to learn what we are designed to do and also to learn how to live the very best life?

Psalm 119 is one of the most powerful testimonies of the richness of the word of God. Verse 105 shows the practical use of God's word to be a lamp and light for our path to show us how we should live this life. Without a common standard to live by, it's no wonder there are so many "sparks flying" in marriages, families and any place where people interact!

Just having God's word on a shelf or on your coffee table will not work. God's instructions have to be followed carefully for life to be lived fully to his glory.

Don't get lost in the traffic or ruin your microwave…and be sure to use God's manual when trying to figure out how to live your life!

28

Do Not Judge

"Do not judge, or you too will be judged. For in the same way you judge others, you will be judged, and with the measure you use, it will be measured to you."

Matthew 7:1–2

How easy it is to see the fault in someone else! Most of the marriage counseling Al and I do is initiated because of the problems the husband and wife see in each other. In our own marriage, I find that too often I can look at Al with a critical eye, yet be oblivious to my own shortcomings.

Have you checked your thoughts as you go through a crowd of people? It would probably shock most of us if we could see how judgmental many of those thoughts may be: "I'm not as heavy as she is" or "I would never dress like that" or "I'm glad my children don't act like that" or "He is so arrogant!" Many of our judgmental views come from comparing ourselves with others.

In a group discussion years ago, a man was complaining about his life situation. At the time he was caring for his aging mother in addition to his wife who had a chronic illness. He was feeling overwhelmed by his struggles, conveying that no one could understand how difficult his situation was.

Finally he said, "Even Jesus didn't have to care for a sick wife and mother!" That did it! In my heart I immediately thought, "How dare he think his struggles are more than Jesus' struggles. And what about the rest of us? Does he see me wearing a badge of suffering because we lost three babies?" How quickly my judgmental attitude took control.

Soon after this incident I heard a speaker share a prayer that helped her in dealing with her criticalness toward others. She prayed, "Judge in me, O Lord, the same thing I am finding fault with in my brother."

Somehow, those words seemed to put the mirror right in front of me so that I had to see myself. My heart was immediately cut and softened when I realized how judgmental my attitude was about this brother. Jesus' words in

Matthew 7:2 are clear—we will be judged with the same measure we use to judge others.

Another principle Jesus taught in dealing with others was to take the plank out of your own eye before trying to remove the speck of sawdust in another's eye (Matthew 7:3–5). Recently I heard an example of this on a radio commentary *Character Counts* in which Michael Josephson told of a time several years ago when he was asked to talk about ethics with the entire California Senate. A senior staffer commented that it was good that Mr. Josephson was addressing that topic since "people lie a lot up here." The staffer quickly added, "I hardly ever lie!"

His comparing himself to others around him whom he viewed as frequent liars made him feel superior. He would have said they had the "plank" in their eyes. Such distorted, judgmental thinking does blind us to our own sins. We do need to check ourselves first before we are quick to condemn others.

Rather than justifying ourselves by finding someone who is worse than we are, we are called to follow Jesus, keeping our eyes on him. He is our example; he is the one we are to imitate. Not only does Jesus tell us not to judge, he also tells us what the standard of judgment is.

In John 12:48 Jesus said,

"There is a judge for the one who rejects me and does not accept my words; that very word which I spoke will condemn him at the last day."

When I measure myself by God's word first and use it as his standard, it humbles me and gives me a clearer view of others.

29

❧

Fear vs Faith

❧

"Why are you so afraid? Do you still have no faith?"

Mark 4:40

Fear can paralyze. Fear can make your blood run cold. I remember a time in our early days of marriage when Al and I were house-sitting. The house was in a beautiful location, somewhat remote, with lots of trees providing extra privacy. After being away for a few hours, we returned to the house, finding the door open when we were sure we had closed it.

As we went through the house, we noticed glasses left in the sink. (I was certain I had not left them there!) We were second-guessing ourselves at every turn until we went into the master bedroom. On the bed was a sword belonging to one of the sons who had gone to a military academy! That was a time I understood what it meant for your blood to run cold!

Now we were sure someone had been in the house, and we had to call the police. Many hours after the police came to check everything, we still did not have any clues as to the culprit. Needless to say, the rest of our stay there was unnerving.

It wasn't until months later we found out that the son had come home from school with one of his friends, had something to drink and showed his military sword to his friend. It would have been nice if he had left a note!

As in many cases, this event shows that often our greatest fears are ungrounded even when facts seem to prove the fears.

There are times when fear can act as a warning for us, but the kind of fear that most of us deal with does more harm than good. Statements like this are not uncommon: "I'm afraid something may happen to my child." Or "I'm afraid someone may break into our home." Or "I'm afraid I have an incurable disease." Or "I'm afraid I will lose my job."

We live in uncertain times with more bad news than we can imagine staring us in the face. We may have quicker access to bad news today, but history makes it clear that for centuries people have faced terrible times.

The Bible is full of God's people facing catastrophic situations, yet over and over God gives his solution. To Abram in Genesis 15:1 God said, "Do not be afraid, Abram. I am your shield." In Genesis 26:24 God spoke to Isaac: "Do not be afraid, for I am with you."

After God strengthened Moses, Moses encouraged the Israelites with,

> "Do not be terrified; do not be afraid of them.
> The LORD your God, who is going before you, will
> fight for you." (Deuteronomy 1:29–30)

This is a great example of one person's faith giving courage to others.

God spoke similar words to Joshua,

> "Be strong and courageous. Do not be terrified;
> do not be discouraged, for the LORD your God
> will be with you wherever you go." (Joshua 1:9)

Jesus comforted his disciples in very uncertain times with, "Do not let your hearts be troubled. Trust in God; trust also in me" (John 14:1). Jesus gave the answer to fear; it is faith—real trust in God and trust in Jesus.

Recognizing God's presence with us keeps us from being controlled by our fears.

As Jesus walked with his disciples, he wanted them to realize that they did not need to give in to fear because he was with them. His disciples witnessed so many evidences of Jesus' power—his healing many with various diseases, driving out demons, cleansing a leper, instantly causing a paralyzed man to walk! Surely they must have had great faith. In Mark 4:38-40 we see otherwise.

In the face of a storm at sea, the disciples frantically awaken the sleeping Jesus with, "Teacher, don't you care if we drown?" Jesus' presence did not calm their stormy fears. In fact, they had already jumped to the worst case scenario—drowning!

What a strong rebuke Jesus gave them: "Why are you so afraid? Do you still have no faith?"

No faith? Fear had so overtaken them that their faith was nowhere to be seen. Mark's account of this event really made me see that fear and faith do not occupy the same space. *Where fear comes in, faith goes out! But where faith comes in, fear goes out.*

It is encouraging to recognize that keeping our eyes on Jesus and his power will strengthen our faith and help us overcome our hysterical fears. Memorizing this powerful statement of faith might help us fight our fears:

When I am afraid,
    I will trust in you.
In God, whose word I praise,
    in God I trust; I will not be afraid.
What can mortal man do to me? (Psalm 56:3-4)

30

❀

What About

My Feelings?

❀

You women who are so complacent,
    rise up and listen to me;
you daughters who *feel* secure,
    hear what I have to say!
In little more than a year
    you who *feel* secure will tremble.
                    Isaiah 32:9–10 (emphasis mine)

Morris Albert's song about a lost love, "Feelings," is still familiar today and expresses the power of our emotions.

Feelings, nothing more than feelings,

> Trying to forget my feelings of love.
> Teardrops rolling down on my face,
> Trying to forget my feelings of love.[1]

Our feelings can be so strong. What do we do with all our feelings? We may want to forget them, but they seem to take control. We women often have an overabundance of them! We are very tied to our emotions. If I feel something, that feeling seems to be connected to who I am.

An often-heard statement is, "I can't help the way I feel!" In other words, my feelings are allowed to define me.

To some of us, feelings equal truth. One person may say, "I feel healthy, so I must be healthy" only to later learn that she has a serious illness.

A woman recently shared with me, "I feel like God doesn't really love me—I know that's not true, but that is the way I feel."

Another may think, "I feel close to God, so I must be saved," not recognizing that God's truth will be the judge, not one's feelings.

It is important to recognize the place of feelings. Our emotions are God-given and are great gifts when under God's control. On the other hand, our emotions can be dangerous when unleashed and not guided by God. It has

---

1. Morris Albert and Gaste Louis Felix-Marie, "Feelings," performed by Morris Albert.

been said that feelings are not right or wrong; but what we do with them can certainly lead to right or wrong.

King Saul is an example of a man driven by his emotions. Early in his kingship his thoughts and his feelings controlled him. In 1 Samuel 13, King Saul foolishly offered up a burnt offering rather than waiting for Samuel as God had commanded. When Samuel confronted him, Saul replied, "I thought, 'Now the Philistines will come down against me at Gilgal, and I have not sought the Lord's favor.' So I felt compelled to offer the burnt offering."

Later in 1 Samuel 18 the attention and acclaim shown to the young man, David, sparked Saul's strong feelings: "very angry," "galled," "jealous eye," and "afraid" (vv8–12). Saul's feelings went unchecked, leading him to try to kill David, and eventually they cost him his throne.

I learned an important lesson about jealous feelings years ago. Dianne was my best friend, but I began to notice that she was also close to some of the other women in our group. If I observed her having deep talks with someone else, I would feel left out and concerned that she might feel closer to that person than to me. Of course, that made me miserable and actually helped me to identify my sin of jealousy.

Once I saw where my feelings were leading me, I really

tried to conquer them. I remember one particular time when I was going into a women's meeting; I knew it was a set-up for me to be tempted with jealousy. Before I went into the meeting, I prayed that God would help me not to give in to that sin. Immediately, I thought, "What if I have those same jealous feelings?"

I then decided to claim the victory ahead of time. Satan was not going to win this round. Not only did I claim the victory, but I told Satan he could have my feelings—I intended to have the thoughts and actions of Jesus, no matter what I felt!

To this day, I remember winning that battle by God's strength. Satan wanted more than my feelings; since he didn't get my actions, he didn't mess with my feelings either.

Most of us do not have a problem with the happy, positive feelings—it's the sad, mad, down feelings that are hard to control. I heard a suggestion on a talk radio program that was helpful. Since feelings are real, it is good to express them then dismiss them. In other words, don't let feelings control you. It is not healthy to stuff them or to talk about them incessantly, but having a safe place to express what you are feeling can lighten your burden.

Another saying I have heard is that feelings should be the caboose, not the engine. Our actions, based on faith and grounded in the truth of God's word, should come ahead of our feelings. When I determined to have the right actions rather than to give in to jealousy, righteous feelings followed.

31

The Fear of God

The fear of the LORD is the beginning of
knowledge,
but fools despise wisdom and discipline.
Proverbs 1:7

There is something about the ocean that draws me.
Maybe it is the vastness of it, or the constancy, or the color
of the water or the sound of the waves. It must be all of
that and more!

Al and I love living close to the ocean. We love it so
much that we usually choose a night away or a vacation
time by the ocean! As much as I am drawn to the ocean,
I am well aware that I do not want to get too far into it.

We like to swim and snorkel, but I'll stay on the beach

if the waves are too high, or the undertow is too strong. I would say I have a healthy fear of the ocean; it can easily overpower me!

When I think of the true fear of God, I get a glimmer of understanding in comparing it to the way I feel about the ocean. Fear of God does not mean I am quaking-in-my-boots scared of him. It is described much more in terms such as awe, respect, amazement, wonder.

It helps to consider some of the qualities of God such as his greatness: "Is anything too hard for the LORD?" (Genesis 18:14). "Is the LORD's arm too short?" (Number 11:23). "Who has measured the waters in the hollow of his hand, or with the breadth of his hand marked off the heavens?" (Isaiah 40:12). "And these are but the outer fringe of his works" (Job 26:14).

God is timeless and his greatness is really indescribable! His holiness is complete; his wisdom is limitless.

One of the most practical definitions to me of the fear of God is understanding who God really is and understanding who I really am. We see this in living color reading the interaction between God and Job in Job 38–41. Just a sampling of the challenges God gave Job are in Job 38:4—"Where were you when I laid the earth's foundation?" and Job 38:12—"Have you ever given orders to the morning or shown the dawn its place?"

Those two questions alone would stop any of us. Job's response was to put his hand over his mouth and say no more! He began to see who God really is and to understand how small he was in comparison.

It would be overwhelming if the fear of God placed an unreachable gap between us. Part of understanding the true fear of God is to accept his infinite love—the love he displayed on the cross through Christ, who made it possible for us to have a relationship with this unfathomable God.

The psalmist expresses this clearly in Psalm 130:3–4 (emphasis mine):

> If you, O LORD, kept a record of sins,
>   O LORD, who could stand?
> But with you there is forgiveness;
>   therefore, you are *feared*.

In addition to the fear of the Lord being the beginning of wisdom and knowledge, there are other benefits:

> The fear of the LORD adds length to life,
>   but the years of the wicked are cut short.
> (Proverbs 10:27)

> The fear of the LORD is a fountain of life,
>   turning a man from the snares of death.
> (Proverbs 14:27)

Through love and faithfulness sin is atoned for;
    through the fear of the LORD a man avoids
        evil.
(Proverbs 16:1)

The fear of the LORD leads to life:
    Then one rests content, untouched by
        trouble."
(Proverbs 19:23)

Humility and the fear of the LORD
    bring wealth and honor and life.
(Proverbs 22:4)

Finally, one last reason to be sure we truly fear the Lord is found in Isaiah 33:6 (emphasis mine):

He will be the sure foundation for your times,
    a rich store of salvation and wisdom and
        knowledge;
    the fear of the LORD is the key to this
        treasure.

We can have the key to God's amazing treasure! When the true fear of God is present in our hearts, overwhelming gratitude will be the obvious response.

❦

32

Wait for God

Yes, LORD, walking in the way of your laws,
we wait for you.

Isaiah 26:8

For young children, waiting can be torture! "How long till we get to Grandma's?"…"When will the movie start?"…"Is Christmas nearly here?" As parents we do our best to help them with the waiting. We play games, we give them treats, and we make calendars for them to mark off the days till Christmas.

As adults, is waiting much easier? It probably depends on what we are waiting for…and maybe how we were trained (or not) to wait when we were children. We live in an "instant" world. We want everything now and fast.

The saying, "I want patience, and I want it right now!" too often describes the way we live.

Recently a song from our girls' younger days came to mind when we were with our granddaughters in Arizona. Their mother (Keri) and I started singing,

> Have patience, have patience,
> don't be in such a hurry.
> When you get impatient,
> you only start to worry.
> Remember, remember
> that God is patient too.
> And think of all the times
> when others had to wait on you!

I'm not sure the granddaughters liked hearing it at the time any more than their mom wanted to hear it as an impatient child. Some things don't change very much from generation to generation.

In my relationship with God there have been times when I must have seemed like an impatient, spoiled child to him. It might have been a request that I didn't think was answered soon enough or in the right way, or a problem that wasn't solved when I wanted it to be.

If I picture myself "kicking and screaming" in front of God, I imagine God shaking his head, saying, "Gloria, Gloria, just stop it! I am in the process of answering your prayer in the best way!" That is a humbling thought!

Another scenario I have imagined is God saying to me, "Okay, Gloria, you tell me exactly what you want to happen, and I will do it exactly your way." The thought of that scares me and helps me wait on God. I've seen some of the results of doing things my way.

Waiting on God does not mean sitting down and "twiddling my thumbs," or doing nothing. The scripture in Isaiah 26:8—"Yes, LORD, walking in the way of your laws, we wait for you"—helps clarify the wait. We are to do the righteous things we know to do, and waiting on God is one of those righteous things.

One of my favorite scriptures is Psalm 85:13:

> Righteousness goes before him
> and prepares the way for his steps.

When we do our part walking in the way of righteousness, we are going in God's direction—that is the path he walks on. He will do his part in his way in his time! Al has a saying that seems to be supported by that scripture: "God doesn't move a parked car."

Are you waiting on God? Start moving with him step by step on his righteous path.

33

❧

Thoughts on Marriage

❧

Marriage should be honored by all.
                        Hebrews 13:4a

When our oldest daughter, Staci, was about to marry Andy Yeatman, he asked what advice I would give him. My response was to love God most, then to love each other more that you love yourself. Marriage seems to bring out our selfishness more than any other relationship.

Another piece of advice Al and I give to couples getting married is to pray together daily. We call this the "spiritual glue" of our marriage. It is our way of starting and ending the day, saying "Good morning" and "Good night" to God together.

Here is some more input I want to give on marriage:

Priorities—My top relationship is to my spouse, second only to God. Once children come into the picture it is too easy to let them take priority over your husband. I have said that we love our children better when we love our spouse best. We are showing our children what a marriage is to be.

Decisions—Since love is a decision, a couple can decide for their marriage to be as great as they want it to be. Even before we were married, we made the decision that we would keep the specialness in our relationship by such things as holding hands, greeting and saying goodbye with a kiss, kissing after we prayed, and saying, "I love you" frequently. We decided that there would be no "back door" for us.

Communication—Good communication takes place when what is said is heard the way it was intended. I need to take responsibility for what my husband hears me say, not just what I actually say. It is important to play back what we communicate to each other in order to be sure that what we say is heard the way it was intended. Al says that any gaps we leave in communication, Satan loves to fill. Of course, that filler is negative, so all the more reason to be sure what we hear is what is really being said.

Friendship—A wife and husband should be each other's best friends. It is important to enjoy doing things together and creating special memories. By being thankful and appreciating each other's differences, we can be our husband's biggest fan instead of his biggest critic.

Respect—Giving my husband respect is God's expectation for me as a wife; it is not an option. The hard part is to be sure that I respect my husband in ways so that he feels respected. We need to treat each other in the family with at least as much respect as we would give a stranger...and much more!

Submission—We are to "submit to one another out of reverence for Christ" (Ephesians 5:21). However, wives in particular, are to submit to their husbands "as to the Lord" (Ephesians 5:22–24). Submission has nothing to do with superiority and inferiority. Godly submission is for godly order. Submission is like a YIELD sign at an intersection—it is to avoid a collision! The wife is not to be silent in her opinions and is not to be a "door mat," but she is to honor God and her husband's leadership by yielding with a willing heart to her husband.

Resolving Conflict—It helps to remember that we are on the same side, not enemies. Do not let issues build up; try to resolve differences quickly. Humility is a necessary ingredient in conflict resolution. Try to understand what your spouse is feeling. Agree to "fight fairly"—not threatening divorce, no name calling, not holding on to the past, not blame shifting, and certainly no physical abuse. Exercise self control—even if you disagree in public (I don't encourage that!), you should work out your differences in such a way that it would not be embarrassing for others to hear you. You do have self-control if you can drive a car. You don't go racing through a stop sign; you brake the car at a red light, then step on the accelerator when the light turns green. You can use self-control in your marriage as well!

Righteousness—Each of us must be committed to righteousness, willing to do the right thing no matter what the other person does. I must realize that my response is my responsibility; I will answer to God for my attitudes and actions. When I do what is right, it takes that much sin out of the equation. I can make a difference in my marriage!

Example—Your marriage will affect others, especially your own children. You are modeling for them what marriage is. What kind of model are you giving them?

Great marriages don't just happen. It takes work to have a deep, loving relationship that will last. You can determine whether you want your marriage to be like weeds or like roses. Weeds grow without any effort and can ruin the good plants around them. Roses, on the other hand, require extra care, feeding and pruning, and the results are breath-taking.

With God's help we can have incredible marriages. I think I will choose the roses! What about you?

34

❦

Thoughts on Parenting

❦

Bring them up in the training and instruction of the Lord.

Ephesians 6:4b

Through the years, many younger mothers have asked me for advice about parenting. While I am very thankful to share some of the things I have learned through the years (often from the "School of Hard Knocks"), I am also sobered about giving advice about parenting. Since each child is unique, no one method or style works with all children.

Also, I have lived long enough to see the trends about child rearing change a number of times. We were raising our girls during the Dr. Spock era, only later finding out that some of his theories were not the best. I am sure that many of you have not even heard of Dr. Spock since other "experts" have replaced him.

Fortunately, we knew there were principles that we could depend on to be effective and unchangeable from the one true expert—God. I can be confident in sharing God's truths with other parents and can also relate some practicals which were helpful to us.

Here are some of the thoughts I have shared:

- Be the adult; be the parent!
  There will be a time later when you can be their best friend.

- Two essential keys to parenting are
  Being unified—In areas of opinion it would be better to do something that may not be the best choice than to choose the best option but not be united.

  Being consistent—Children will be confused if parents are not consistent. Imagine how confused a driver would be if one day it was legal to stop at a red light, but the next day he got a ticket for stopping at the same red light. It is easier to be consistent if you make as few rules as possible, but enforce those rules implicitly.

- Practice what you preach.
  Make God the center of your home in a genuine
  way. Children are like little video cameras, recording everything. They learn by example. You don't
  want to raise little hypocrites!

- Model respect and expect respect.
  What a person says and does is of prime importance in communicating respect, and the person's
  tone of voice and body language also play an essential part.

- In general, the mother sets the tone for the home.
  "If Momma ain't happy, ain't nobody happy!"

- Tips from my mother:
  You will love your child, but no one else will unless
  you teach them to be obedient and respectful.

  God gave children to parents to teach the parents
  rather than the other way around.

- Obedience
  Our children use this guideline with their children:
  "First time, every time, and with a good attitude."

We learned that counting "1…2…3" actually teaches the child he doesn't have to obey till you get to "2½."

- Teens
  If you wonder what your child will be as a teenager, look at him at two then multiply by eight, and you have a sixteen year old!

- When they want to talk, be ready to listen.
  Don't react! Try to understand what they are feeling and expressing.

- Enjoy every stage.
  Children grow up so fast! Be sure to treasure the times you have with them. Make memories to be cherished for years to come.

- Vision
  The key to your vision for your family in the future is your vision for your family *now*!

It is comforting to know that we do not have to be perfect parents. We will make mistakes. We and our children will learn and grow through them—not be ruined by them. God is the ultimate Father who is molding and shaping all of us. He will work even through mistakes if we are humble toward him and others, and if we keep loving our children. Love does cover a multitude of sins.

35

Take Captive Every Thought

We take captive every thought to make it obedient to Christ.

2 Corinthians 10:5

Research has shown that we can speak approximately 120–180 words per minute, we can listen or hear approximately 400 words per minute, and we can think approximately 800 words per minute. Is it any wonder that there is so much miscommunication? With so many thoughts going through our minds, we can get side-tracked with something that has not even been said!

In addition to the actual words being said, we are also

aware of the tone of voice being used, the look on the speaker's face, and many other non-verbal cues. Our thoughts are quickly recording these things, many times subconsciously.

I have discovered that in addition to recording the words heard and the non-verbal things I observe, I frequently add my own private commentary (usually negative). The difficult aspect of this is that it happens so quickly that I am rarely even aware of what is going on in my mind.

I have heard it said, "It's not what people think about us that is the problem; it is what *we think* people think about us that causes the difficulty." I have a vivid personal example of this.

A number of years ago Al and I thought it would be fun to get some exercise together by playing racquetball. Al is very athletic and had played racquetball for some time. I, on the other hand, am not athletic and was a beginner. Before we even started playing, I was feeling insecure due to my inexperience and wondered if Al would enjoy playing with such a novice. To my surprise it was a lot of fun for both of us. Al was very patient and helped me as I learned.

Then one day he suggested that we try a different approach to our practice. At this point my thoughts were,

"I knew this would happen—he needs some variety to not get bored playing with me. I play like a baby compared to him!" My own insecurities took over, and instantly, all the fun was gone for me. Of course, I didn't tell Al what I was thinking, but my actions and attitude communicated loudly. We didn't play much longer that day!

Later as we tried to unravel what had happened, I shared my feelings and thoughts. He quickly reassured me that his suggestion was only to help me and had nothing to do with changing practice to avoid boredom for him. This experience was a stark example to me of how my own thoughts can be so wrong and can even sabotage something good.

Our minds can be like a tape recorder with a negative tape set and ready to play. It is all too easy to hit the "Start" button and let it go. It is vital to remember that there is a "Stop" button as well, and you can also erase a tape!

In 2 Corinthians 10:5 Paul gives us the key to victory over negative thinking: "...and we take captive every thought to make it obedient to Christ." This means we have to be alert to what is going on in our minds rather than just letting our thoughts run rampant.

Taking something captive implies expending a lot of effort, energy and strength. You may have to wrestle it down to the ground and put it in hand-cuffs. If it is difficult to capture our every thought, it is even more challenging to make it obedient to Christ.

Thankfully, through prayer and meditating on God's word, we receive the power of the Spirit to shape our thinking into that of Christ's. Only with his help can we begin to take on the mind of Christ (1 Corinthians 2:16).

36

Challenge for a Lifetime

Be completely humble.

Ephesians 4:2a

I have read the book of Ephesians numerous times, but as I read chapter 4 this particular time, I could not seem to go past the first three words in verse 2: "Be completely humble." It was the word "completely" that grabbed my attention. There are some times when I can be humble, but "completely" means completely—all the time. That is challenging!

One area of struggle that I recognized at that time was to exercise humility when Al corrected me. It was easier for me to take correction from someone else (not that I always handled that well, either). My defenses would quickly go up if Al pointed out something I needed to change.

Sometimes I would verbally defend myself making excuses, or I would try to point out to him how he had done something wrong too. At other times I might not say anything, but my silence conveyed anything but an attitude of humility—probably because I was defending myself in my heart.

I decided then to have Ephesians 4:2 become my theme scripture for that year. I might as well confess now that one year was not long enough; I extended it to the next year—and then the next. Yes, now I consider it the challenge for my lifetime.

My only hope for deep and lasting change in this area is to constantly strive to imitate Jesus who was completely humble. In

Philippians 2:6–8 Paul says of Jesus,

> Who, being in very nature God,
> did not consider equality with God something
>   to be grasped,
> but made himself nothing,
> taking the very nature of a servant,
> being made in human likeness.
> And being found in appearance as a man,
> he humbled himself
> and became obedient to death—
> even death on a cross!

Humility on the outside must start with humility on the inside. Jesus' attitude and his very nature epitomized humility. Complete humility cannot be exercised depending on the circumstances. Circumstantial humility might sound like this: "If Al had said it in a different way, then I could have been humble." Other words I have said are: "I started out trying to listen and be humble, but then I felt attacked."

Jesus' example again is so convicting. When he was attacked most viciously and accused falsely, he said nothing! (After I wrote this, I leaned back and said, "God, help me!!") It is a lifetime challenge.

Later I remembered a very encouraging promise of God: "God opposes the proud but gives grace to the humble" (James 4:6b).

Prior to Paul's description of Jesus' attitude, Paul gives some practical instruction to help us imitate Jesus' humility:

> Do nothing out of selfish ambition or vain conceit, but in humility consider others better than yourselves. Each of you should look not only to your own interests, but also to the interests of others.

In the footnotes of the *NIV Study Bible* for Philippians 2:3, selfish ambition and vain conceit are called the "mortal enemies" of unity and harmony in the church. In contrast humility is noted to be the source of Christian unity. The comments regarding "consider others better than yourselves" are helpful as well: "Not that everyone else is superior or more talented, but that Christian love sees others as worthy of preferential treatment." No wonder being completely humble is so necessary.

Humility is displayed in many ways; one evidence of it that I want in my life is the attitude of being a lifetime learner. I don't want to ever get to a point that I think "I've arrived." There are always new things for me to learn. Recognizing that I do not know everything keeps me open to learning from others. I believe there are valuable things I can learn from anyone—no matter their age, background or status. A person does not need to be an "expert" before I can learn from him.

Maybe one reason Jesus called us to be like little children is that they are eager to learn. Learning lessons from every situation we face helps us to mature, yet to keep a youthful spirit.

While I can see that there has been some growth in my humility through the last few years, the "completely" part will continue to call me higher as I strive to imitate Jesus. Maybe you'll join me in this lifetime challenge!

Closing Thought

It can be exciting to get older. If you don't think so, just ask our four-year-old grandson, Cameron. A few days before his last birthday, I said, "Cameron, you are almost four!" He quickly responded, "Then I'm almost five; then I'm almost six!" I must confess that my response to my recent sixty-seventh birthday was not the same as Cameron's.

Growing older has a lot to do with perspective and attitude. I've heard it said that the kind of older person you become will be the kind of younger person you were. I cannot help getting older, but I don't have to be "old." I am happy to be sixty-seven! I want to make the most of the life God gives me, learning lessons from every experience and then sharing those lessons with others. I want to be God's "pitcher."

Other Writings

The following writings are chapters I wrote in several anthologies published by DPI. I offer these as added resources and encouraging helps. Note that some of the facts are out of date because these chapters were written several years ago.

Building and Sharing Family
The Fine Art of Hospitality

"Home is where the heart is." Building family begins in the heart. Family hits at our emotions—our deep roots. As I thought about building family, I first tried to recall how Al and I built our family. But soon my thoughts went back to my own childhood and experience of family as I grew up. I was surprised at the flow of tears that came as I remembered our home and family—Mother and Daddy, my older brother, David, and later my grandfather and cousin, Billy, who came to live with us when my grandmother died. My tears were mixed with thankfulness and sadness—thankfulness for the rich heritage of love I have been given; sadness because I lost my mother this past January and with her death came a sense of losing "home."

As long as I can remember, family also meant lots of uncles, aunts and cousins plus a continual flow of people of different nationalities who came either to visit or to live with us. We did not live in plush surroundings, but when people came to our home, they were genuinely loved and welcomed with warm hugs and homemade chocolate chip cookies from my mom's well-known cookie jar. Interestingly, after Mother's death, one of my most prized keepsakes was her cookie jar. Though of very little monetary value, it is a cherished symbol to me of our family life.

To some, remembering family can bring tears because of hurts, pain, neglect and abuse. Today's family must be described with added words such as "traditional," "nuclear," "dysfunctional," "single-parent," "composite," "blended," etc. Discipling is a universal principle that works. We will be like our parents in both good and bad ways. Often family traits, habits and traditions are carried on without even realizing it. Fortunately, when we are born into God's family, God gives us a new heart and reshapes our view of family according to the truth of his Word. Our part in this reshaping is being open and eager for training and continual input.

Closeness in Immediate Family

As Al and I began our marriage, we consciously imitated aspects of my parents' relationship that we admired: praying together, having daily devotionals, saying "I love you," showing affection (kissing "hello" and "goodbye" and after mealtime prayers). Those early marriage habits set the tone for a solid spiritual and emotional base for Al and me and our three daughters. From their earliest years we taught and expected our girls to be close to God, to us as their parents, and to each other.

Close to God

For our children's hearts to be totally devoted to God we must pray for them before they are born and continue to pray for them and with them afterwards. In Deuteronomy 6 God's command to teach and train our children as we go about our daily routine is the key to a spiritual family. Some of our best talks about God and his love and care were in the car as I drove the girls from place to place, and at night as they were getting ready for bed. Their deepest thoughts and biggest concerns seemed to come out more easily at those relaxed times.

Dinner time proved to be the best time for us to pull our family together. It was a time to turn off TV, ignore the phone, share special events or problems of the day, and focus on God and lessons from his Word. Weekly family devotionals were great training times for the girls to pray aloud, lead favorite songs and to plan and present lessons. We memorized Bible verses that we remember to this day, and we frequently played Bible games. These times were vital to show how to implement God's principles practically in their daily experiences.

Close to Parents

The most significant factors that pulled our family close, next to our love for God, were our love for each other as husband and wife and our unity as we trained our girls. Never underestimate the power of outward expressions of love and affection between parents. Although our girls acted embarrassed at our kissing after our mealtime prayers, now our married daughters and their husbands (and many other couples around the world) have made that a habit too. Most importantly, our loving each other as husband and wife second only to God, gave our girls security and trained them to love their husbands above their children.

In training and disciplining children, unity between parents is key. At one time or another all three of our girls tried the "divide and conquer" technique with "But Dad said I could…" or "Let's ask Mom. She'll let us…" When they saw our unified stance or were aware that we worked through any differences to a point of unity, they ultimately felt secure and loved, though maybe disappointed initially.

We learned all sorts of life lessons helping the girls with their physics and calculus, working in the kitchen together, planting and tending the garden, going to the emergency room for stitches, selling Girl Scout cookies, and tearfully burying our little dog, Buttons. It is vital to make the most of the time spent together and to be available and accessible. Parents need to be alert to the times and situations in which each child is the most open and eager to talk—then be available.

Close to Each Other As Siblings

Our family was close in more ways than one. We lived in a small three bedroom/one bathroom house during our girls' growing-up years. Interestingly, what we would consider a disadvantage today really was an advantage in training our girls to cooperate, share and repent of selfishness.

Al and I had an expectation for our girls that they love— *and like*—each other. I often reminded them that sisters can be friends. We treated them with respect and demanded respectful interactions first with us and then with each other. For instance, saying "Shut up!" to someone was not allowed. Our family nights were special memory-making times. We took turns choosing what meal we wanted, and the girls often worked together to prepare it. A favorite choice on a snowy night was cheese fondue served by the fireplace followed by a devotional and a game of Aggravation.

Extending Family to Others

One of the richest blessings of having strong family ties is bringing others in, whether short term or long, to share the love and warmth. In Matthew 25:34–40 Jesus makes it clear that when we care for others, we are caring for him. We had to open up our home by first opening up our hearts! We have seen God enrich our lives through every person who came into our home. Not every experience was a positive one, but even then we learned some very important lessons.

Doing the best with what you have is a vital principle in extending family to others. We could not refuse to invite people into our home because we did not have a spare bedroom or an extra bathroom. Typically one of the girls' bedrooms was designated as a guest room and could quickly be rearranged for anyone coming to stay with us. The bathroom schedule certainly had to be planned out and communicated to everyone involved. We all remember a youth rally weekend when around twenty girls stayed with us, and yes, with one bathroom! I think they really felt family!

There is no better place for learning and growing than having people live with us. We all are seen and see each other in action daily. Just as we taught and trained our girls on a daily basis, so we have had opportunity to teach and train others in basics such as cooking, cleaning and budgeting. As we included them in our lives, they experienced family devotionals, fun times, our daily time with God and our interactions—"bumps" too—and we saw theirs as well.

We have had people of all ages and backgrounds stay with us: children whose parents couldn't care for them, several people with emotional instabilities, teens off the street, families with young children, families from other countries, singles without jobs, very stable and responsible singles, married couples with severe problems and strong, spiritual couples. All the different people who have been in our home are intertwined in our lives and hearts in a very special way. We have more "children" and "grandchildren" than we would ever have imagined!

What a responsibility and privilege we have as Christians to communicate God's sense of true family in today's world! Family makes a difference! Family gives us a belonging place! As we build family God's way, we will radiate love and support which will draw others to him—and to the church, his family.

Sheila Jones and Betty Dyson, *The Fine Art of Hospitality* (Spring Hill, TN: DPI, 1995). The original book is no longer in print. However, a newer abridged copy is available from DPI.

Marriage: True Companions
First...the Kingdom

> "It has been said, 'Anyone who divorces his wife must give her a certificate of divorce.' But I tell you that anyone who divorces his wife, except for marital unfaithfulness, causes her to become an adulteress, and anyone who marries the divorced woman commits adultery."
>
> Matthew 5:31–32

Irreconcilable differences. Incompatibility. Mental anguish. On-paper reasons for divorce. In-the-heart reason? "I just don't love him/her anymore." Jesus' teaching on divorce is strong. It challenges the fickleness of human nature. A spoiled and pampered people don't know the definition of faithfulness and integrity in the marriage relationship.

Because of its teaching on divorce, the Bible is dismissed by many. In the United States and other countries the word "divorce" is as commonly used as "marriage," and is widely accepted and even encouraged. Interestingly, human nature has not changed much in two thousand years. In one of their confrontations with Jesus (Matthew 19:3), the Pharisees tested him by asking, "Is it lawful for a man to divorce his wife for any and every reason?" In that day a man could divorce his wife if she did anything he disliked—even if she burned his food while cooking it! The husband cried the first-century equivalent of "irreconcilable differences" and got a new wife.

Jesus' response is found in Matthew 5:31–32 and in 19:1–9. In the latter passage Jesus lays the foundation for his teaching on divorce—God's original and perfect plan. One man—one woman—one lifetime. God's way works! Complete faithfulness in marriage. Go in the front door of marriage and keep the back door shut. Go in with a mind-set of giving of yourself, of meeting his/her needs, of working through conflict, of staying put through the rough times, of not giving up.

Marriage As an Analogy

Faithfulness. If we truly have it in marriage, we must first have it with God. The Scriptures repeatedly draw a parallel between marriage and our relationship with God. As Jesus recalled God's plan for marriage from the beginning (Matthew 19:5, Genesis 2:24), he used the word "united." Romans 6:5 conveys the reality of being "united" with Christ in his death and in his resurrection. The *oneness* in marriage is also stressed in our relationship with Christ—"for you are all one in Christ Jesus" (Galatians 3:28). Paul in his letter to the church in Ephesus uses the identical statement found in Genesis 2:24 and Matthew 19:5 in his instructions to husbands and wives. Then in Ephesians 5:32 he clarifies the correlation, "This is a profound mystery—but I'm talking about Christ and the church."

Unfaithfulness in marriage is also unfaithfulness to God! 1 John 4:20 says "…for anyone who does not love his brother, whom he has seen, cannot love God, whom he has not seen."

In much the same way, how can man claim to be faithful to God and not be faithful to his spouse? This principle is clear as God communicates his displeasure through Malachi 2:14, "...the Lord is acting as the witness between you and the wife of your youth, because you have broken faith with her, though she is your partner, the wife of your marriage covenant." It is amazing to see how integral God's spiritual principles are to our human relationships. Our faithfulness to him is mirrored in our faithfulness to our husbands/wives.

Marriage As a Model

In a time when half of all marriages end in divorce (and even more couples are emotionally divorced) what a privilege it is to be disciples of Jesus. Disciples whose marriages can be used by God as lights and examples. Godly models of strong marriages are more vital than ever. I am eternally grateful for the example of my parents' God-centered marriage of sixty years. Their devotion and love for God and each other continue to inspire my husband, Al, and me as we grow in our marriage. As our daughters marry, we see the incredible impact of discipling. And now, at the recent birth of our first granddaughter, we envision the plan for great Christian marriages going on and on.

What kind of model is your marriage? Is it a model of faithfulness or unfaithfulness? Nothing tests our marriages like seeing the reality of discipling lived out in the marriages of our children and others watching us. We may not realize that we are teaching others through our marriages. But we are—either positively or negatively. Praying together has been the spiritual "glue" that bonds our marriage. Daily prayer has kept us open and vulnerable to God and to each other. Our unity of heart, mind and purpose have been intensified in those special times together.

Do you want others to imitate the unity and oneness in your marriage? Are you working as a team, or do you have your own separate agendas? There are times Al senses "resistance" from me is some area. Disunity in our team hurts us both. If we get "off-track" emotionally or sexually, it weakens our effectiveness as a team and makes us more vulnerable to Satan's temptations. If either of us loses our concern for others, the strength of our unity is lessened. Unity can be destroyed by unresolved conflict, bitterness, lack of forgiveness and just plain apathy.

Satan desires to strike deadly blows to our faithfulness. He eagerly goes after it. Daily. Always. No vacation. Only as we choose to adhere to God's standard will our marriages bring glory to God.

At weddings, the question is "Will you forsake all others and be faithful till death parts you?" At divorces, the judge asks, "Is your marriage irretrievably broken with no hope of reconciliation?" Many have said, "Yes!" to the first question. Half of those have also said, "Yes!" to the second question. The fullness of the tragedy is that so many in both groups have never said, "Yes!" to God. They have not built their marriages on a foundation of true faithfulness.

Disciples of Jesus, who have been made new through the blood of Christ, can joyfully and gratefully say, "Yes!" to being faithful in marriage. Daily. Always. Forever.

FOR FURTHER STUDY:
Deuteronomy 24:1-4
Hosea 4:10-14
Malachi 2:13-16
Mark 10:11-12
Luke 16:18
Hebrews 13:4

Jones, Thomas and Sheila, eds. *First the Kingdom* (Spring Hill, TN: DPI, 1994). This book is available from DPI.

The Sage of the Ages
The Wisdom of God
Our God Is an Awesome God

God's wisdom—infinite! Immeasurable! Unlimited! Inconceivable! Unfathomable! Just after I wrote these words, a sister called me to get some "words of wisdom." My response was, "I am writing a chapter on God's wisdom; I've got a very humble view of my wisdom right now!" In reality I should always have that view. God is omniscient—all-knowing. He is the source of all knowledge and wisdom.

God's Wisdom Displayed

The wisdom of God is magnificently displayed in creation.

> By wisdom the LORD laid the earth's foundations,
>   by understanding he set the heavens in place.
> (Proverbs 3:19)

God's wisdom is seen in the amazing foresight and preparation that went into making a world suitable for human beings. Before each of our three girls was born, we eagerly planned and worked to have the nursery decorated, the crib in place and baby clothes, diapers and bottles ready. How much more did God in his unlimited wisdom prepare for the birth of his children! From God's first act of creation, we see him readying the "nursery" before man was even made. His initial command, "Let there be light" (Genesis 1:3), began his preparation for us. You see, we need light; God does not—as David acknowledged in Psalm 139:12—"even the darkness will not be dark to you; the night will shine like the day, for darkness is as light to you." Furthermore, we need day and night; God does not—I marvel at God's plan to renew our strength and energy while we sleep at night. What an ingenious design! How often we take God's work for granted.

In his wisdom, God created the world in such a way that it helps us to understand who he is. For example, consider the ocean. It possesses a calming force, reminding me of the vastness of God's knowledge and the constancy of his love. Prayer walks along the beach put me back in touch with God's perspective as I surrender my burdens to him. Or think about—as Jesus urged us in Matthew 6—the birds of the air and the lilies of the field. Seeing how God takes care of these little creatures helps me to fight anxious thoughts and feelings. Al and I are currently in the midst of another move and are looking for a place to live. Certainly the Creator of the universe can meet our housing needs!

God's Wisdom Personified

The stark contrast between God's wisdom and the "wisdom" of man is clearly described in 1 Corinthians 1:22–25:

> Jews demand miraculous signs and Greeks look for wisdom, but we preach Christ crucified: a stumbling block to Jews and foolishness to Gentiles, but to those whom God has called, both Jews and Greeks,

> Christ the power of God and the wisdom of God. For
> the foolishness of God is wiser than man's wisdom,
> and the weakness of God is stronger than man's
> strength.

The world is groping for answers to life's many questions. God's emphatic answer to our questions is Jesus. The wisdom of God is personified in Christ. His life, death and resurrection respond to our deepest questions in a way no textbook or philosophy ever could. Without Jesus, our "wisdom" is nothing more than blind foolishness.

The Beginning of Wisdom

If we ever want to truly understand God's wisdom, we must go "back to the beginning":

> The fear of the LORD is the beginning of wisdom,
>   and knowledge of the Holy One is understanding.
> (Proverbs 9:10)

It is sad to see the pain and devastation caused when we ignore God's wisdom. Working to help people involved in all types of sins, I have often found myself asking, "Where is the fear of God?" More and more, I am convinced that this is a missing piece in the heart of too many disciples. They only think of the fear of God as being afraid of God's anger and punishment. While that is a part of it, the most vital aspects are missing—reverence, awe and respect. We can't begin to know the wisdom of God until we understand what it is to fear him.

One of the defining examples of the fear of God was Job's encounter with him. After a few questions from God, Job was quickly put in his place. God challenged Job to answer his questions:

> "Where were you when I laid the earth's
>   foundation?
>   Tell me, if you understand."
> "On what were its footings set,
>   or who laid its cornerstone?"
> "Have you ever given orders to the morning,
>   or shown the dawn its place?"
> "What is the way to the abode of light?
>   And where does darkness reside?"
> (Job 38:4, 6, 12, 19)

Totally humbled, Job finally replied to the Lord:

> "I know that you can do all things;
>   no plan of yours can be thwarted.
> You asked, 'Who is this that obscures my
>   counsel without knowledge?'
>   Surely I spoke of things I did not understand,
>   things too wonderful for me to know."
> "My ears had heard of you
>   but now my eyes have seen you.
> Therefore I despise myself
>   and repent in dust and ashes."
> (Job 42:2–3, 5–6)

Simply defined, the fear of the Lord is seeing who God is—*really*—and seeing who I am—*really*! We must see the gigantic chasm that exists between God's righteousness and our sinfulness. The fear of God brings us to humility and gratitude as we recognize that only the sacrifice of Jesus can bridge that chasm for us. The person who fears God is motivated to trust him, to live his life in obedience to him and to avoid sinning.

In his book, *The Joy of Fearing God*, Jerry Bridges gives several characteristics of a God-fearing person. He lives his life under the authority of God, acknowledging that Jesus is Lord and helping others to do the same. He is conscious of the presence of God, as well as of his dependence on God. Fearing God means living to the glory of God, desiring to honor and please him in all things above self and others.

Studying about the fear of God and striving to practice it daily has changed my life. I have reexamined my motivation—why do I share my faith? Why do I want to be fruitful? Why do I serve others? What will keep me pure and honest when no one is looking? The fear of the Lord truly is the beginning of wisdom.

The wise man Solomon, after examining his life and the lessons he learned, said:

> Now all has been heard;
>   here is the conclusion of the matter:
> Fear God and keep his commandments,
>   for this is the whole duty of man.
> (Ecclesiastes 12:13)

As we embrace the God of all wisdom and Jesus Christ, who is the wisdom of God, we become part of God's master plan for our lives. Now that is good news worth sharing!

Questions:

1) What is your real attitude toward God's wisdom as compared to your wisdom? How is this demonstrated in your speech and actions?

2) Is your perspective of God's wisdom in creation different than your perspective of God's wisdom in your daily life? If so, how?

3) In what ways do you see the wisdom of God displayed in Jesus' life, death and resurrection? What questions of yours did God answer by sending Jesus?

4) What does the fear of God mean to you? Why is this an important motivation for you in living your life for God?

Kelly and Dede Petre, eds. *Our God Is an Awesome God* (Spring Hill, TN: DPI, 1999). This book is available from DPI.

Dealing with Miscarriage
Life and Godliness for Everywoman, Volume One

A loss is a loss! Whether it is an early-stage miscarriage, a premature baby who doesn't survive, a stillbirth, an ectopic pregnancy, an in vitro fertilization that doesn't work, or not being able to get pregnant at all—a loss is still a loss. In any of these situations there is a deep sense of emptiness that is very painful and difficult to understand and accept. It seems the more advanced the pregnancy is or the longer you have a child with you, the harder the loss. However, when you personally have to face a loss, comparisons do not matter, it just hurts!

I know this firsthand—Al and I lost our first baby, a boy born seven weeks early who lived three days. What a shock it was and how much it hurt. He would have been the first grandbaby on both sides of our family; suddenly everything was different. I remember realizing how vulnerable we were— bad things could happen to us. We had to face something we did not like and did not understand. Our faith was tested like never before.

It is vital to be able to feel and to express the hurt. This does not mean you have to "fall apart," but you need to express your emotions and be very real. Stuffing your feelings or trying to "keep a stiff upper lip" will possibly prevent or at least lengthen the healing process. Al and I naturally asked "Why?" yet we soon realized we could not demand the answer. We had to talk through our feelings and questions with each other and with people close to us.

We also learned that we had to allow each other to react differently to our loss. Many times the husband is less emotional, especially in an early-stage miscarriage because the pregnancy is not as real to him as it is to the wife. She is undergoing all the physical and hormonal changes, so will probably be very emotional. It is important to talk about the different feelings and reactions so that neither person makes wrong assumptions (examples: she doesn't have faith; he doesn't care). In the Garden, Jesus modeled the handling of intense emotions (Matthew 26:36–46). He was incredibly open and vulnerable, yet didn't lose control. He drew his friends in closely and shared his most intense feelings even when they did not provide much support. He chose to rely on God and to surrender to his will. Al and I could not change the fact that our baby son died, but we could choose to hold on to God and his promises.

About this time an older woman taught me a vital life lesson. She said, "It is not important what happens to you, but how you act and react to situations, persons and things that makes all the difference." We determined to grow closer to each other and to God through our loss.

Throughout our lives we will all face challenges. God continually works to teach us to trust him. For Al and me, losing our first baby was a major testing ground in our learning to trust God, especially when it hurts! The alternative to trusting God is to distrust him. We could kick and fight against God and blame him for our hurt, but that would not bring our baby back. It would leave us void of the comfort, love and peace that

God provides when we do trust him. We continually marvel at God's power when we think back to hard times and remember how he brought us through them. God does provide incredible strength just when you need it.

More Loss and More Joy

After this loss I had a sense that surely we had had our share of hardships. However, pain and hardships do not come in "fair" doses by our definition and understanding. My second pregnancy went well and even though our daughter, Staci, came five weeks early; she was healthy and strong.

When she was nearly two, I was pregnant again. At about six and a half months into my pregnancy I went into premature labor and delivered twin girls (a total surprise to us—before the days of ultrasound!). Our excitement soon turned to sadness as both of them died about a day after they were born. How could this be happening again? We asked, "Why?" but again had to choose to trust God through the hurt and the questions.

As God strengthened us, we realized that our strength had to help others. Ironically, we had to be strong for the people around us. We had to let them know that we could talk about our losses—that we would not fall apart if someone talked about babies or brought a baby around us. Comforting others probably enabled us to work through the pain in a healthier way.

One of the things that helped us after our losses was to get pregnant again as soon as the doctor thought it was safe. That certainly helped to fill the void we felt and also gave us hopeful anticipation of another baby. Before I could get pregnant after we lost the twins, I had to have corrective surgery for an incompetent cervix, which also meant that I would have Caesarian sections with any other births. God blessed us with Kristi about a year later. She arrived a month early after an emergency C-section.

Three years after Kristi was born, I delivered Keri, five weeks early, also by emergency C-section. Then Keri started having breathing trouble and we thought we were going to lose her (the babies we lost had all had respiratory difficulties). I remember being in despair struggling with God and saying I couldn't bear losing another baby and going through that agony again. That was a landmark "wrestling with God" time that I will never forget. I was finally able to surrender to God's will remembering how he had carried us through the other losses and knowing he would be with us again.

At that same time Keri was in an ambulance being taken to Boston Floating Hospital to get specialized treatment. The nurse with her on the ride reported that Keri had a marked change for the better, enough so that the receiving physician at the hospital asked why she was being brought there. We call Keri our "miracle baby," and I believe surrendering to God played a part.

It is amazing to see the things we learn through our hardest times. We also learn through difficulties others have—especially those closest to us. After our "miracle baby" Keri grew up and married Steve Hiddleson, Al and I were thrilled to hear that they were expecting a baby. Because of the problems I had with our babies, my trust in God had to go to new levels as my daughters have been pregnant. Things had gone well in Keri's pregnancy until the seventh month—she noticed that she had not felt movement for several hours. An ultrasound showed that their baby boy had died; he was delivered stillborn the next day.

It is one thing to go through something yourself—it is quite another challenge to watch your children go through hardships. We were so proud of Keri and Steve as they relied on God and trusted Him. God faithfully provided incredible strength for them just as he had done for us.

That was four years ago. Al and I recently went to see the Hiddlesons in Kansas to celebrate the third birthday of their daughter, Sierra.

Time Eases the Pain

What a difference time makes! Although the loss is never forgotten, time eases the pain and helps the healing process. One of my favorite verses, Psalm 31:14–15, says "But I trust in you, O LORD; I say, 'You are my God.' My times are in your hands." It is important to know it is okay to be happy again. Some parents feel they are being disloyal to the baby they lost if they don't hold on to some measure of sadness. God is able to heal us so we can be completely happy, yet forever changed.

Looking back over the years, I can see God's molding and shaping of our character through the hardest of times, as well as the best of times. Only God knows what kind of people Al and I would be had we never experienced loss. We do know that we are different because of what we learned. We are amazed at the opportunities we have to help and "comfort those in any trouble with the comfort we ourselves have received from God" (2 Corinthians 1:4).

Really learning to accept something that you do not like and that you do not understand is a major part of trusting God. It took me years before I could step back and see that the only way we could have six children in heaven for eternity was for things to happen just as they did. God's perspective is so much greater and all-encompassing than ours. We are so caught up in the here and now, but God's ultimate focus is eternity.

Helping Those in Grief

Here are some practicals to help a grieving person:

- Each person's loss is unique; the way each person handles grief and loss is unique. Don't say, "I know exactly how you feel" even if you have had a similar loss.
- Be a good listener. Help draw out their feelings.
- Be compassionate and feel with them. "...mourn with those who mourn" (Romans 12:15).
- What you say is not as important as what you do—being there, giving hugs, helping with meals and ordinary tasks.
- Do not be afraid to talk about the loss, but do be sensitive to the feelings and reactions of the grieving person.

- Realize that grief comes in waves. The bereaved person will not "just get over it" quickly. Their world has forever changed.
- Be there longer than just the week or two around the loss. Life goes on very fast for everyone else, but it feels like it has come to a crashing halt for the one experiencing the loss.
- Be spiritually focused. Pray for and with the person.
- Do not be too quick to give pat answers even if they are correct, such as "we know that God works all things for good," or "you can always have another baby," or "you can still adopt," or "at least you have your other children," etc. There will be the time and place for right answers and advice, but if it is thrown in immediately, it seems to smooth over the hurt insensitively.

Sheila Jones, ed. *Life and Godliness for Everywoman, Volume 1* (Spring Hill, TN: DPI, 2000). This book is available from DPI and offers a whole "library" of helpful articles for various aspects of women's lives.

Contentment vs Worry
Life and Godliness for Everywoman, Volume 1

What do contentment and worry have in common? Absolutely nothing! In fact, they cannot co-exist. Women struggle a lot with worry; it seems we come by it naturally. An article on psychotherapy entitled "Are we better yet?" (LA TIMES – 1-18-00) had this to say about worry: "We have created whole new categories of what people should worry about, hundreds of new ways in which we can fail or people can fail us."

Worry is sin. We must fight against it. We are in a battle, and one of our biggest battlefields is in our own thoughts! We will never win the battle over worry until we take responsibility for our thinking and "take captive every thought to make it obedient to Christ" (2 Corinthians 10:5). Who and what feeds your thoughts? It is important to evaluate our views and thoughts about ourselves, our roles and our relationships. This will help us to win the battle against worry.

Yourself
Your View

- Comparing with others
  This causes so much discontentment—worry about being tall or short, having straight hair or curly, being athletic or artistic, having big feet or small feet, etc.
- Wondering what others think of us
  The problem is more what we *think* others think about

us. We can be totally wrong, and then respond as if the person actually is thinking a certain thing about us.

- Looking at ourselves
  We can over-react to aging, wrinkles, extra pounds, etc. This is often just part of the normal aging process.
- Who feeds your thoughts? The world or the Word?

God's View: Psalm 139:1–4, 13–16

- God created your inmost being
- What do you need to do with your emotions, your feelings? Express them, then dismiss them. They should be the caboose rather than the engine.
- Praise God and thank him for your uniqueness.
- Choose to believe God and take responsibility for your thoughts and actions.
- Do your part to be your best as with diet, exercise, etc.

Your Role
Your View

- "For we are God's workmanship, created in Christ Jesus to do good works, which God prepared in advance for us to do" (Ephesians 2:10).
- Will I ever…? Get married? Have children? Be in the ministry?
- What if…? I get in a wreck? Have cancer? My child gets hurt?
- I'm not as important since I no longer lead a Bible talk. Since I no longer lead a sector. Since the leader isn't dis-

cipling me anymore.
- "Grass is greener" attitude—someone else's situation is always better or more desirable.

> It was spring but it was summer I wanted; the
> warm days and the great outdoors.
> It was summer but it was fall I wanted; the colorful
> leaves and the cool dry air.
> It was fall but it was winter I wanted; the beautiful
> snow and the joy of the holiday season.
> It was now winter but it was spring I wanted; the
> warmth and the blossoming of nature.
> I was a child but it was adulthood I wanted; the
> freedom and the respect.
> I was twenty but it was thirty I wanted; to be
> mature and sophisticated.
> I was middle-aged but it was twenty I wanted; the
> youth and the free spirit.
> I was retired but it was middle-age that I wanted;
> the presence of mind without limitations.
> My life was over but I never got what I wanted.[1]
> (written by a fourteen-year-old boy)

God's View: Psalm 16:5–6
- Be thankful for God's plan and purpose for your life.
- Love each phase of your life; enjoy the gift of singleness, the gift of motherhood, etc.
- Choose to be content.

---

1. Linda Dillow, *Calm My Anxious Heart*, (Colorado Springs, Co.: NavPress, 1998), 101.

Your Relationships

Your View of Your Relationships

- Do you have expectations such as: "When I get married, my husband will…? My parent should…? My Christian sisters should…?

- How do you handle disappointments, hurts, etc? (Worry? Shut down? Get bitter?) One of the biggest tests of contentment comes when something you do not like happens or you do not get something you want. (Philippians 2:14: "Being discontented with God's will is an expression of unbelief that prevents one from doing what pleases God."–from the *NIV Study Bible*)

God's Perspective of Your Relationships – Ephesians 4:31–5:2–32

- Be open about your negative and sinful feelings toward others.

- Get help after you have been open—don't just "dump and run" and excuse your sin.

- Choose to imitate God's forgiveness and sacrifice in your relationships.

God's view is always the truth. Any view that we have that differs from God's view is not truth. And the truth certainly sets us free to be all he intended us to be.

Sheila Jones, ed. *Life and Godliness for Everywoman, Volume 1* (Spring Hill, TN: DPI, 2000). This book is available from DPI and offers a whole "library" of helpful articles for various aspects of women's lives.

Comments in "As Our Parents Age"
Compilation Chapter in
Life and Godliness for Everywoman, Volume Two

It seems to me that this is one of the hardest stages of life. There are so many variables and so many aspects that are unpredictable. From my experiences I would offer the following suggestions:

- After losing three of our four parents, I am sure of one thing: you do not regret time spent with them. I don't think I have ever heard anyone express regret about spending too much time with their parents. Defining how and when to spend time with them is difficult given our active lives and many responsibilities. We are so grateful for the input and advice we were given at those times. Thank God for discipling!

- If at all possible, it is best to have heart-to-heart talks with your parents about their wishes for this stage of their lives. It is wise to write those desires and plans down in order to follow them as closely as possible. Shortly before my mom died, she and my dad talked about what he would do after her death; then they shared their thoughts with us children to discuss. It helped so much to know that we had all agreed ahead of time that my dad would come to California to stay with both my brother and his wife and with us.

- One of the most important aspects of caring for your

parents in the latter years of their lives is to work closely with any siblings we have. It helps to share the load of the various decisions that must be made as well as to share in the actual care of your parents if possible. The communication between siblings and their spouses is very important—especially drawing out and being open about the feelings each has. The more you cooperate and can be on the same page, the better things will go.

Sheila Jones, ed. *Life and Godliness for Everywoman, Volume 2* (Spring Hill, TN: DPI, 2001). These comments are from a longer chapter on this topic. The book is available from DPI.

Eunice and Lois
Faithful Forerunners
She Shall Be Called Woman, Second Edition,
Volume Two

Acts 14:8–23; Acts 16:1–5; 2 Timothy 1:5; 3:14–15

A visit from Zeus and Hermes—the lead Greek god and his spokesperson. That's what the Lystrans thought was happening when Barnabas and Paul arrived during their first missionary journey. After they performed the miracle of healing a man born crippled, the people concluded that surely this was a visit from the gods. Sources indicate that an ancient legend told of a visit by the two gods. In the legend, only one poor couple welcomed them, so the whole city was punished for their lack of hospitality. Obviously, the people of Lystra did not want to make that mistake again and suffer those consequences. After finally dissuading the people from sacrificing to them, Paul and Barnabas preached the message of Jesus for the first time in a Gentile area.

After some time, Jews from Antioch and Iconium came over to stir up trouble for them (a six- or seven-day journey by foot). They were successful in their mission, and as a result, Paul was stoned and left for dead. Whether he was resurrected or just revived is not clear, but God certainly worked miraculously to allow him to be on the road again with his companions the next morning, going to Derbe to preach. Among the people who responded to the message and became disciples in Lystra was Eunice, a Jewess with a heart for God, and, in all likelihood, her mother Lois as well.

———————————

The time had come—the time for which she had spent years preparing—the time for Timothy to leave home. She, as well as her mother, Lois, and her teenage son, Timothy, eagerly anticipated Paul's return to Lystra after several years of waiting. Yet, she was unprepared for Paul's request that Timothy accompany him on his travels. She was familiar with Paul's travels—how vividly she remembered his first time in Lystra. It was a time that changed not only her life but also that of her mother and son for eternity! As she strained her eyes to get one last glimpse of Paul and her young Timothy before the road curved out of sight, tears welled up, her throat tightened, but her heart was full of joy and gratitude. Memories came flooding in...

Unequally Yoked

The birth of a son! What exhilarating happiness Eunice felt as she held this precious gift from God. At the same time, she was sobered knowing that his spiritual training would mostly be her responsibility. What joy she felt, seeing how proudly her handsome Greek husband looked at the tiny bundle in her arms. What thankfulness that her mother—now a grandmother—was there to support and strengthen her, to pray with her. She needed to rely more on God than she ever had.

Naively, Eunice had thought that the addition of a child to their mixed marriage would produce little conflict. Her husband's Greek and heathen background were seemingly unimportant to him while her own Jewish faith in the one true God and his holy Scriptures was preeminent. She was unprepared for his reaction as she suggested the name Timothy, signifying "one who fears God." She could still remember being stunned by her husband's complete resistance to circumcising their son on the eighth day according to Jewish law.

Wisely, Grandmother Lois had urged her to entrust this baby son to God and prayerfully and willingly to be submissive to her husband. Eunice couldn't help smiling as she realized how many times she had put that same advice into practice. How powerfully God had answered and honored those prayers and actions!

Train Up a Child

As Eunice recalled those early days of Timothy's life, she remembered the pact she and Lois had made to do all within their power to train him in the fear of God and in the knowledge of the Scriptures. A Jewish boy formally began to study the Old Testament at age five, but Timothy was taught by his mother and grandmother at home at a much earlier age. During those years, young Timothy had frequent bouts of illness and yet, was never too weak to enjoy hearing the

Scriptures read. It delighted him to surprise Eunice and Lois by reciting the scriptures he had committed to memory! Even his father, though an unbeliever, was amazed and inwardly impressed by his son's knowledge and zeal.

Mothers' prayers for their children are probably the most consistent requests brought to God. Certainly this was true for Eunice. Often she and Lois would plead together for wisdom, guidance and extra help so they could train Timothy to be his best for God. She felt her limitations as a woman married to an unbeliever. She knew Timothy needed a strong spiritual male influence. She saw gaps in his development, especially due to his physical illnesses that weakened him and caused him to withdraw at times. Little had she known how God would meet those needs.

Changed for Eternity

Paul! In her mind's eye she could see Paul and Barnabas in the marketplace as clearly as if it were yesterday. Eunice and her mother had just gotten there when they saw a huge crowd of people shouting, "The gods Zeus and Hermes have come down to us in human form!" Immediately, two men rushed out of the crowd tearing their clothes crying out, "Why are you doing this? We too are only men, human like you. We are bringing you good news, telling you to turn from these worthless things to the living God" (Acts 14:15).

On hearing those words, Eunice and Lois worked their way to the front of the crowd, eager to hear what these men had to say about "the living God." What they heard struck their hearts as nothing ever had. THE MESSIAH—their long-await-ed Messiah had come! Jesus of Nazareth came teaching and healing only to be betrayed and crucified!

Tears filled Eunice's eyes as she remembered Paul's convict-ing words about each person's sin being responsible for the crucifying of the Son of God. When that startling reality hit her, she could hardly breathe. She was guilty. What could she do? Yet, thankfully, Paul had told of Jesus' burial and then his incredible resurrection three days later, and hope entered her heart. For Lois and Eunice, time stopped until they made that decision of decisions—Jesus would be their Lord! They would be disciples! Repenting of all their sins, they were baptized into Jesus—into the very kingdom of God! Their lives had forever been changed.

And Timothy? She should have known there would be no way to hold Timothy back. His love for the Scriptures and for God had prepared him to hear Paul's message. Timothy had seen his mother's and grandmother's tears of joy and heard the great news about Jesus. He saw their faith in action and saw changes in their lives like never before. He had to meet Paul and Barnabas. It wasn't hard to find them—just look for the crowd.

What a message! What boldness! What courage! Timothy had never heard a man speak with such forceful convictions. Eunice would never forget what happened next. She and her mother had been right behind Timothy, when out of the crowd, angry Jews from Antioch and Iconium pushed toward Paul. Their taunts and jeers and threats grew louder and spread like wildfire, turning the crowd into an angry mob. They shoved and dragged Paul outside the city where they viciously stoned him.

As quickly as the mob had gathered, it dispersed leaving the seemingly dead Paul in the dirt. By the time Timothy reached Paul, disciples had surrounded the body. Lois and Eunice, out of breath from trying to keep up with Timothy, gasped, "Is Paul alive?" Before Timothy could say "No," he saw Paul getting up from the ground—Unbelievable! Miraculous! The disciples were jumping for joy, crying, praising and thanking God and hugging Paul all at once.

After the initial exuberance, Timothy felt burning tears of shame rolling down his face as he realized his own fear, his lack of faith, his lack of boldness in the face of danger. Eunice knew he was experiencing the same heart-rending awareness of his sins that she had felt when Paul had preached about the cross of Jesus. Nothing could stop him. Timothy—her young son, her young man—became a disciple. Paul's words, "We must go through many hardships to enter the kingdom of God" (Acts 14:22) would be indelibly stamped on their hearts and minds.

God's Answers

Was it just a few weeks ago that Paul had come back to Lystra? So much had happened in a short span of time. Eunice stood in awe of how God had answered her prayers. She could not have asked for a more spiritual man than Paul to disciple her son. Paul knew Timothy's weaknesses, but he saw his potential and had great vision for him. Timothy's eagerness to accompany Paul on his travels was evidence that God had answered prayers for growth in his boldness and courage. Timothy certainly had seen firsthand what hardships meant. And Timothy's circumcision—it hadn't happened when he was eight days old, but it did happen before he left with Paul. God used even that to help her trust his timing. And Timothy certainly learned a new level of trust in God—and in Paul, who did the circumcising (Acts 16:3)!

As Eunice turned back to the house after Paul and Timothy disappeared from her sight, Lois came to meet her. As they embraced, no words were spoken. Their tears came again, and in their hearts they shared a deeper faith than ever. Somehow they knew this faith, this trust would be tried and tested in the months and years to come. They could be at peace; their son/grandson was in good hands—Paul's, and most of all—God's!

Times of Surrender

Eunice and Lois have come alive through my study. I identify with Eunice as a mother; I identify with Lois as a grandmother. What models of faith they both are! When I thought of Eunice and Lois in years past, I was inspired by their training of Timothy from infancy. Their example especially influenced me in my years of motherhood when our three girls Staci, Kristi and Keri were young. My own parents instilled in me a love for God and his Word from an early age, and I wanted to do that for our girls. Memorizing Bible verses was a regular part of our family devotionals and meal times together. Al, the girls and I would take turns quizzing each other.

Probably the most convicting aspect of Eunice and Lois' lives was their faith. When I have read 2 Timothy 4:5—Paul's words to Timothy of his "sincere faith which first lived in your grandmother Lois and in your mother Eunice"—I have thought in terms of their faith to become disciples and that faith influencing Timothy. Digging deeper into the lives of Timothy, Eunice and Lois has challenged me profoundly as I have thought of the circumstances in which a mother's and grandmother's faith would be tested the most. To realize for the first time that Eunice probably witnessed Paul's stoning in Acts 14; and then later agreed to her teenage son traveling with that same man, fully understanding the persecutions that would face them, *challenged me to the core!* Today, some of us have difficulty "letting go" of our children as they go to school for the first time or spend a night away from us.

A point in my life when I could especially identify with Eunice occurred several years ago when all three of our girls left us in Boston about the same time to pursue mission opportunities around the world. I remember the feelings of concern, loneliness and a certain "emptiness" with all our daughters out of reach. At the same time, I was thankful for the opportunities each of them would have. For me it was a time of growing and maturing as I "untied the apron strings"—one of many times to surrender our girls to God.

My own mother has been a great example to me through the years as she and my dad willingly and prayerfully supported our moving from Texas to Boston (with their only grandchildren). I remembered that model as our daughter Staci and her husband, Andy, moved to Italy. That challenged the "almost-grandmother" role in me, because Staci was pregnant and would deliver our first grandchild in an Italian hospital. God continues to prove his love and cares for us and honors our faith and surrender to him. He has blessed us with a beautiful granddaughter, Kiara, now a year old and a little closer to us in Boston.

God has placed so much power in the hands of women—to build up or tear down. Through the years I have developed what I call my "open hands prayer." As fear, anxiety and worry tempt me, I consciously, physically open my hands in prayer to God, releasing everything to his care and will. There are times when the struggle to control is so strong that I have to open my hands again and again to surrender fully.

Whether mothers, grandmothers, wives or singles, the challenge is to be faithful women who will continually surrender every area of our lives to God. Now hundreds of years later, though very little was written about them, the example of Eunice and Lois motivates and inspires us like never before!

Focus Question:

Which word describes your approach to life—control? or surrender? What or how do you need to surrender today?

Linda Brumley and Sheila Jones, eds. *She Shall Be Called Woman, Vol 2, Second Edition, New Testament Women* (Spring Hill, TN: DPI, 1998). This book is available from DPI along with vol 1 (Old Testament women).